LUCKY GIRL

Lessons on Overcoming Odds and Building a Limitless Future

SCOUT BASSETT

Nashville • New York

Worthy
Hachette Book Group
1290 Avenue of the Americas, New York, NY 10104
worthypublishing.com
twitter.com/worthypub

First Edition: September 2023

Worthy is a division of Hachette Book Group, Inc. The Worthy name and logo are trademarks of Hachette Book Group, Inc.

The publisher is not responsible for websites (or their content) that are not owned by the publisher.

Worthy Books may be purchased in bulk for business, educational, or promotional use. For information, please contact your local bookseller or the Hachette Book Group Special Markets Department at special.markets@hbgusa.com.

Library of Congress Control Number: 2023016032

ISBNs: 978-1-5460-0386-1 (hardcover), 978-1-5460-0388-5 (ebook)

Printed in the United States of America

LSC-C

Printing 1, 2023

For all the girls who've ever been told you can't win in life.
They were wrong.

CONTENTS

INTRODUCTION

I was born in Nanjing, China, where I was given the name Zhu Fuzhi, which means *Lucky Girl*. I have looked back many times on my life and found great irony in the meaning of my name.

Because if we're talking about luck, mine's been pretty bad.

As an infant, I was involved in a fire that resulted in the loss of my right leg. After being abandoned in the streets of Nanjing, I was taken to a government-run orphanage where I spent the next seven years living off one bowl of rice a day, leaving me at twenty-two pounds—the size of a toddler—at eight years old. I didn't worry about finding a family. I worried about staying alive.

The amputation of my leg was botched. I wouldn't be surprised if I found out it was done by the local butcher. In time, a bone (probably a left-behind growth plate) extruded from the back of my thigh, making a prosthesis anatomically incompatible with my body. Not to mention it hurt like hell. The best the orphanage could do was give me a homemade prosthesis connected to my body by four leather straps—straps that with every movement inflicted licks of fiery pain along the skin of my remaining leg.

I can't speak for the other children in the orphanage, but this is my experience and what I personally witnessed.

The orphanage was not a safe place for me. It wasn't safe for any of the kids there, but especially those of us with limb differences. You think it's difficult to navigate America as a disabled person? My orphanage didn't have money to keep our stomachs full. To discuss building out any sort of accommodations for me or the other kids with disabilities would have sounded like the punch line to a bad joke.

I was known to fall—often—in the trough-style bathrooms, which were brutal to navigate hopping on one foot. Because, believe it or not, I'd rather have hopped or scooted across a nasty bathroom floor than endure the agony of ripping open new sores using my makeshift prosthetic. For the most part, I used my hands and left leg to crawl or scooted on my bum to navigate the world around me.

Speaking of the world around me: My childhood "home" was, in every way, a prison. The floor was made of a dark wood, but I never actually saw it. Despite our scrubbing it day in and day out, the floor was so old and stained that it appeared to be covered in black tar. We slept two to a bed. Though, "bed" is a generous word for the narrow cots we were given. There was no air-conditioning in the orphanage, and the nights would get unbearably hot. We'd argue with one another about who "got to" sleep on the filthy floor. But if we got caught *not* in our beds, the punishment was brutal.

Speaking of punishments, the most common form of consequences for the kids in the orphanage was waterboarding. Waterboarding is when someone uses water to bring you to the point of drowning without actually letting you drown. I remember having my head shoved in water so nasty, I couldn't see through it when I opened my eyes. I remember being so disoriented when they waterboarded me that when they pushed my head under the water, I didn't know which way to struggle toward for air.

The orphanage was dark, crowded, and fueled by fear. I was sentenced to almost eight years of hard time there. We didn't go outside once. I had no context for the outside world and thought every kid grew up the way I did. Until I came to the United States, I'd never seen an animal. Not just in person, but ever. We had no TV, no books, no school. Just work.

Then, just like *that*, I was whisked away on an airplane to the United States to be adopted by a white American family from a small town in northern Michigan.

I know what you're thinking:

Now that's luck! Adopted at eight years old by an American family?

You probably imagine I was thrilled to leave behind my life of loneliness, hopelessness, hunger, and pain. You probably think I was elated to have a mother and father and siblings after years of being cared for by underpaid government employees. You probably think that I finally felt like the *lucky girl* I was named to be.

But the farther behind me China became, the more homesick I got, and the heavier my heart sank into my gut. Even when an environment is toxic, if it's familiar, if it's all you've ever known, it's terrifying to let it go.

I was filled with dread. In hindsight, I realize that what scared me was mostly the unknown. I had context for the orphanage. And even though I knew it wasn't what was best for me, it was still home in the sense that it's where I belonged. I knew how to survive there. How to fit in. Crossing an ocean, going to a country where I didn't know the language or the culture—would I find my place in America?

It was almost like I sensed the challenges that faced me across the Pacific.

I left Nanjing as Zhu Fuzhi, the unluckiest "lucky girl," and I arrived in America as "that Asian girl with one leg," Scout Bassett.

This isn't the part of my story where I tell you my life turned around. No, that wouldn't come until later, when I was fourteen years old and received my first running prosthetic.

After being tossed into the American experience, what came next for me were many years of identity crisis. The private Christian school my adoptive parents sent me to felt unaccepting and non-inclusive to me. As the only Asian in the entire school (Asian *and* disabled), I felt the other kids (and most adults) treated me as beneath them—as less than. As an *other*. As a newcomer to a town of sixteen hundred people it isn't hard to feel ostracized. It isn't hard to feel like an outsider—to *know* you are an outsider.

I yearned for relief from the weight of my pain: the physical pain of a poorly amputated leg and the emotional pain of what appeared to be an amputated future.

Because of the obviously difficult circumstances surrounding my life, the odds—my "luck"—felt stacked against me. Stacked on top of me, really. I wasn't given a level playing field on which to start life. If anything, I was coming from a deficit. But eventually, I was given a leg up. Or, at least a leg.

When I was in eighth grade, I received a running prosthetic from the Challenged Athletes Foundation. At the time, my goal was only to have a prosthetic that didn't make a farting noise every time I stood up. That's right—imagine being in middle school and every time you stand up, it sounds like you're passing gas. It was every adolescent girl's nightmare. Actually, it still sounds pretty bad now that I'm in my thirties.

When I got this new leg, I realized two things: (1) I couldn't hide anymore. The C-shaped blade would be impossible to disguise. I would finally be *seen* by the world as a disabled person. And, (2) I didn't care. The rush I felt running my first race was more important than the false sense of security I had built from pretending to be "normal."

See, up until that point, I believed the perceptions others had of me. That I was worthless and would never be successful, that I would never be loved or accepted. But the first time I stood on a track and heard the gunshot that signaled my first race? I found my way to beat the odds—my way to have a limitless future. I was no longer an *other*. I was *me*. And if finding *me* meant being an *other*, I knew I would risk everything to be her. Running didn't make me feel necessarily lucky, but I did feel empowered to change the odds I had faced at every turn in life up until that point.

This began my journey to embrace who I am—past and all—never forgetting where I've come from or what I've gone through, but leveraging those experiences to fuel my passion and my purpose. When I started running, it was a season of self-actualization. I decided almost immediately that I was done with the cosmetic cover that "disguised" my prosthetic. That I was done hiding. That I was done trying to be like the other kids. And that I was done feeling sorry for myself.

I realized I needed to embrace who I was—to embrace my story. I decided I wasn't going to be ashamed of the things that had happened to me as a child, or ashamed of being an amputee, or ashamed of being Asian. Instead, I was going to lean into those intersections and maybe even celebrate Scout Bassett. Running was really that transformative for me. I grew in confidence; I grew in self-belief. I held my head just a little bit higher. I'd found freedom.

I hadn't had the tools yet to accept who and what I was, but running helped me find those. I deserved better. I deserved more. And I was determined to become a voice for others like me who had suffered because they were different.

Over the years, my experiences have led me to become a professional athlete, Paralympian medalist, world-record holder, ambassador, philanthropist, and mentor. Sport is my passion. But championing those who struggle to be seen, heard, and valued is my purpose.

Maybe you feel unlucky. Maybe you feel as if you've been set up to fail. Your home life sucks. Or you don't fit neatly into one social scene. You've been rejected. Your dreams feel impossible. You've experienced discrimination or have been marginalized. Or maybe you long to be loved, but you fear putting yourself out there, so you remain in a cycle of self-protection and isolation. Maybe you feel unlucky because everyone keeps telling you how very lucky you are, but all you feel is a lack of something you can't name. Or even worse, you just feel numb most of the time.

We've all gone through seasons of life when we've felt disappointed, discontented, rejected, abandoned, or like we're an outsider. That's right—all of us. The most popular girl at school, the most successful female athlete, and the highest-powered woman in business. We've all felt like the odds are stacked against us.

I hear you. I am you. I've struggled against the tides of adversity my entire life, dealing with its challenges and the issues of identity that confront us all.

But over the course of my career, I've been able to come alongside young women from all over the world, all levels of ability, from various demographics and economic backgrounds, of all ages. I see the pain you're in. I see the odds you're up against. I've been there. But I've learned some invaluable lessons—most of the time, the hard way—over the last thirty-some years of life. And I want to share those lessons with you.

Lessons on some of the most common and most challenging adversities we face in a culture like ours, lessons on…

Bad luck.

Being an "other."

Unmet expectations.

Loneliness.

Body image.

And then lessons on strategies I've used in my own life to overcome adversities, like…

Your why.

The comeback.

Building your team.

Your influence.

Being a champion.

Maybe, like me, you don't have an older sister or an aunt or even a mom you can talk to about these kinds of things. That's okay. I didn't either. That's why I'm writing this book. It's meant to be a guide for what you're going through right now, and for what you might be going through in the near future.

We're all born with a set of limitations—of odds. Maybe you were born with a learning disability or physical impairment.

Maybe your family has lacked stability or you live in an area where there aren't many people who look or think like you do. Maybe you never fit in at school, or maybe school was always difficult for you. Maybe you have faced mental health obstacles—depression, anxiety, or even a diagnosis like ADHD, dyslexia, or bipolar disorder.

We're all faced with challenges in life that are beyond our control. But our reaction to those challenges, the strategies we use to approach them, give us the ability to change those odds. To position ourselves to be overcomers—to be champions.

My vision for our relationship is to inspire you to have the fortitude, the grit, the strength, and the mental toughness to do just that.

The most important outcomes, the biggest wins in life, have nothing to do with medals or records or grades or status. They have to do with our commitment to believing we have the power to overcome, to persevere, and to become who we were created to be—more than a lucky girl, but a girl with a limitless future.

CHAPTER ONE

BAD LUCK

H ere's the thing about luck.

I believe in luck.

But also, I don't believe in luck.

Let me explain.

GOING UNNOTICED

Growing up we went to this hardware store down the street from my house owned by a man who attended our church. He had a three-legged cat named Tres that hobbled up and down the aisles, seeking—with some degree of success—the attention and pets of patrons. Like I said, before coming to America, I had never seen a cat or dog before. I want you to imagine that first moment when I saw a furry creature slinking up and down the aisles. I freaked out and hid behind my mom's legs. I didn't have the words yet to articulate what I wanted to say, but it was something to the effect of, "WHAT...HAIRY...WILL EAT ME!"

So, yeah. The first time I saw Tres, it was a little terrifying. But over time, he and I came to an uneasy truce—you don't touch me and I won't touch you. When we saw each other, we would only exchange glances of hello and goodbye.

On one visit to the store, I noticed Tres was missing.

"Where's Tres?" I asked.

The man looked around like I'd spoken, well, Chinese. "Tres? He's...Hmm, I guess he's missing. Now that you mention it, I haven't seen him in a few days."

I was maybe ten or eleven, and I was floored that the guy hadn't even noticed his cat was missing—the cat he shared four walls with every working day.

"Who's Tres?" my dad asked.

"The cat," I clarified. "The cat that's here every time we've ever been here."

My dad shrugged. So did the shop owner.

At my school, I was Tres. Because I was disabled and Asian, I was an oddity that eventually became a comfortable fixture—like a mascot or a store pet. I was different from every other kid in my school or community. If you *did* notice me, it was only because of those differences. But for the most part, I wandered the halls like Tres wandered the aisles, unseen.

If Tres were capable of feeling complex emotions, I bet he'd agree—going unnoticed makes you feel both unlucky and unimportant.

Like Tres, I was completely forgettable unless I did something unexpected…like win a spelling bee.

C-H-A-M-P

Not to brag, but when I was in sixth and seventh grade, I won the school-wide spelling bee two years in a row. I even went on to win the regional spelling bee that second year. I was one word away from making it to the national spelling bee in Washington, DC, but I came up short on "affogato." (Affogato is an Italian dessert made with coffee, and even though it smells like you'd imagine heaven tastes, homegirl refuses to try it on principle.)

I know what you're thinking—*Of course you won the spelling bee, Scout. You're Asian.* We'll get to that. But I'm not your typical Asian—or even the typical Asian American. The first year I won, I'd only been speaking English for about five years—less than half my life. I don't think anyone, including me or my parents, saw those wins coming. I can promise you my classmates and teachers didn't see it coming.

Most of them never saw me at all.

So, how did the Tres of Trinity Christian School become the dark horse of the middle school spelling bee before she was even fluent in the English language? In a stroke of absolute luck, were the handful of difficult words I knew the only ones I was given to spell? I'll let you decide.

When you're twelve and thirteen, all that matters in life are friends. Who is hosting the sleepover Friday, who made the basketball team, who messaged who on social media, what did they say, how could they, and do we still like her now? That's what matters.

Since I didn't have any friends, I needed a way to keep my mind entertained. And you know how they say when you lack one sense, the remaining senses improve? Like how, when you're blindfolded, your hearing sharpens and your sense of taste becomes keener? That's how it's been with the loss of my right leg. My mind has raced to the places my missing leg has been unable to go. For every step it missed, I've had one thousand thoughts. Books, and more specifically, words, became a coping mechanism for me as soon as I could read. (Which, by the way, was far later than the majority of kids in the world, and almost all kids in America.)

I entered that first spelling bee with so much confidence because I knew I had prepared more than anyone else in the entire school. This was before I received my running prosthetic, so what else did I have to do with my idle time and overactive brain? I spent hours every night going down the list of words, studying my Merriam-Webster dictionary, memorizing origins and roots, and writing down tips for each of the words like little cheat codes for ways that would help me to remember how to spell them.

There wasn't a word on the practice list I didn't know how to spell.

I got on that stage knowing that I was ready. That I had done everything I could possibly do to give myself the best outcome I was capable of.

I came to America just shy of my eighth birthday and was stuck in a kindergarten class. And at the time, I still stumbled over usage and sentence structure. The translation of Chinese words to English would sometimes get lodged somewhere between my head and my mouth. To think that I would be capable of winning a spelling bee? The odds were *not* in my favor. Not by a long shot. I didn't even have average odds. I was operating from a deficit.

And yet...I won. Not once, but twice. Was I just lucky?

The words I spelled were words I either remembered or knew how to guess at based on my mental cheat sheet. To that, I guess you can attribute some measure of luck. But the true source of my "good fortune" was my extreme nerd-ism—that's what changed the game for me. In a sense, I redefined my own odds by putting in the work, making the next right choice over and over, and sacrificing my time to raise the ceiling of my potential.

I'm not saying that winning the spelling bee changed my future. But I am saying that I learned a discipline as a preteen that has served me my entire life: If you don't like your odds, change them.

LOTTERY LUCK

Don't get me wrong—I have certainly experienced pure, dumb luck before. That's what I call lottery luck. You buy a scratch-off ticket and win fifty dollars? That's lucky. No strategy involved. No way to improve your odds other than spending more money to buy more tickets. Lottery luck can be significant. In January 2016, three winning lottery tickets were sold across the United States to win the Powerball prize that was valued at $1.59 *billion*. Billion with a "b"!

Now that's luck.

But even in lottery luck, players have to play the game to win. They have to believe that winning is possible for them. And the money they pay to buy a ticket is a sacrifice they make for a chance to win. Are you seeing a pattern?

Let's look at another aspect of luck—the *appearance* of luck.

THE APPEARANCE OF LUCK

I went to school with a girl I'll call Hayley. Hayley was a cliché: blond, cheerleader, smart, and popular. She also had two functioning legs, which is more than I could say for myself. I spent years wishing I could be more like Hayley. *She's so freaking lucky*, I would think, watching her ponytail bob up and down as she talked animatedly in the hallway. *Some girls really do have all the luck.*

When we were in eighth grade, I overheard my parents talking in the kitchen. The word "foreclosure" was mentioned in the same sentence as Hayley's parents' names.

"Wait, what?" I asked. "Hayley's house is going to be fore-closed on?"

My dad nodded. "Her dad's an alcoholic," he said, always to the point. "Looks like he's in jail for another DUI. Won't be get-ting out any time soon. I guess her mom can't pay the mortgage."

That was the end of the conversation, but certainly not the end of my thinking about it. I watched Hayley for weeks after I found out she and her family were getting kicked out of their home and that her dad had gotten sentenced to six months in jail for his third DUI. (I read the local newspaper for fun, too.)

It was difficult for me to conceive that something so incred-ibly bad—so *unlucky*—could happen to someone so seemingly shiny and strong. From my limited perspective, some people were just born with better odds. They were born in the "sun-shine" of life while I was born in the rain. Have you ever felt that way? Like some people are just born with advantages that you weren't? Like some people have all the luck?

That's how I felt about Hayley. In my middle school brain, all that existed was what I could see in front of me. Hayley was always surrounded by other kids who seemed to feel the same way about her that I did. She answered questions in class with confidence. She was pretty. And honestly, she even seemed nice. Which was the hardest part to accept.

But I hadn't learned yet that adversity spares no one in the course of life. I hadn't learned to look for the coping mechanisms, to assume I don't have the whole story, and I didn't have the awareness that none of us are offered perfect odds.

We all have to overcome obstacles in order to create a limitless future for ourselves.

But even as an adult, I'll catch myself in that same middle school mindset. I'll think, *They're so lucky. They get all these opportunities. They have a great family. They have a support system. They have money. They have luck.*

WAVES OF ADVERSITY

I don't know why we tend to do this as humans—look at someone else's odds and tell ourselves that they've got it better or easier than we do. We'll talk a little later about comparison, but I'm a firm believer that any time we compare ourselves to someone else, we all lose. Because we're not seeing each other as people—as humans. Instead, we're seeing each other as lists of often-temporary circumstances.

The truth is we have no idea what another person has been through—or even what they're currently going through. We don't know what demons they've faced, what tragedies they've suffered, or what hardships they've had to wade through. We constantly feel like we're the "only ones" who have the odds stacked against us, but that isn't true. It's actually a pretty selfish mindset, honestly. It's a perception that only takes into account *our* experiences. And it's a limiting perception. If we view ourselves as victims, that's what we are—powerless and without recourse.

If you spend enough time on this planet, and you choose to see life as it really is, you'll learn that our human experience really isn't that different from anyone else's. Not at its core, at least. Adversity comes for all of us. Sometimes in small doses. Sometimes in a rush. But adversity does come, over and over, like waves in the ocean.

When I was in my mid-twenties, I received my first micro-process prosthetic knee, which is basically a computerized knee system. It completely changed my life. I could do things I had never done before, like squatting, climbing up and down steep hills and stairs. But the best part of this new type of knee was that it allowed me to walk into the ocean for the very first time on two feet.

I had read books, heard stories, and watched movies where people either talked about or actually did get caught up in the waves of the ocean. I could never quite understand how that was possible until I was a quarter of a century old, standing in the Pacific, with two feet planted in its sandy bottom.

It's the tide that makes the difference. Not necessarily the waves themselves—until you wade out farther, obviously. But as I stood there, I was surprised by the tug—the pull toward the deeper, more treacherous waters. All while the waves lap against you, coming one after the other, after the other.

I had the thought while I was standing there that the ocean has the same effect on all of us—kind of like life. It doesn't matter how strong you are, what your background is, or your race, economic status, or gender—the waves keep coming, pushing and pulling you.

That's how adversity is. It keeps coming and coming and coming. We'll think to ourselves, *When is this going to stop? When are things just going to be easy?* The answer? Never. Things *can* get better. Things *can* improve. But life will never be easy. And fair? That's not something life promises, either.

Now, before you go thinking I'm about doom and gloom and bad news, I'm not. I'm trying to tell you what I wish someone had told me when I was younger: Adversity doesn't stop. Life isn't easy for anyone, nor is it very fair. But life can still be beautiful, meaningful, and joy-filled *if* you learn to create your own odds.

CREATING YOUR OWN ODDS

I've been a die-hard Braves fan since my childhood summers spent in Atlanta. Like, if the Braves are having a bad season, check on me. Because I am unwell.

But the Braves did *not* have a bad 2021 season. Not bad at all. In fact, the Braves won the 2021 World Series, shutting out the Houston Astros in Game 5, 7–0. But the Braves should have never even made it to the playoffs.

Atlanta entered the postseason with the worst record of any other team still in World Series contention. After a mediocre season with just eighty-eight wins, a season where their best player (and my personal favorite) Ronald Acuña Jr. injured his knee with a complete ACL tear, *and* their best young pitcher tore his Achilles tendon—twice—there was no reason any Braves fan should have expected to see success postseason. In fact, for more than two-thirds of the season, the Braves had a losing record.

If Atlanta would have been in any other division, they wouldn't have made it beyond the regular season. But they did. And they kept winning. Not in a big, sweeping fashion like you see in the movies where a veteran player stands up and gives a rousing speech that unites a previously divided team. Where some 1990s metal riff hits and all of a sudden bats are cracking and gloves are smacking. That's not what happened.

Slowly, there was a shift in momentum. A change in the wind.

The Braves organization took a chance on themselves. In baseball, the season is long—it's a grind. It lasts over a six-month period for 162 games. The World Series takes place in October. There's a trade deadline that usually falls in the last days of summer where teams have one last chance to either offload expensive players in hopes of a better season next year, or buy or trade for players to carry them into playoffs. The decision to buy or sell is absolutely critical. Get it wrong, and you can cripple a franchise for years.

If any team should have been sellers in 2021, it was the Braves. They absolutely should have been punting and looking ahead to Acuña's return and a better roster in the coming season. But guess what? The Braves decided not to be sellers. They decided to be buyers. Because they expected more from themselves. And they closed out the 2021 season with a World Series trophy for the first time in over twenty-six years, breaking the "Heartbreak Atlanta" streak of Atlanta sports clubs. I even got to watch a World Series game in Atlanta, and homegirl had no chill at all about it.

The Braves changed their own odds by betting on themselves. When no one else believed in them, they did. They didn't give up on themselves, even though statistically they should have. And there's a lesson to be learned here. In a post-victory interview, another one of my favorite players, Dansby Swanson, said this about their win: "There were times where it seemed bleak…There were times where you couldn't see the light at the end of the tunnel. But we knew that if we kept working and if we were able to kind of put together a team—which we did after some of the injuries—that this would be possible."[1]

The secret to the Braves' "lucky" win proves that maybe luck had very little to do with it. As Swanson said, "But we knew that if we kept working…" See, the trick is to learn to view obstacles as just that—something to overcome. But as long as you keep working, you don't give up, you still have a chance. You reframe your problems, struggles, and challenges as opportunities to grow. As opportunities to prove others wrong. As opportunities to get the bigger win.

Because maybe the "lucky" people aren't lucky at all. They are people who have learned to create their own odds by refusing to accept the hand of cards they've been dealt in life. The Braves had every reason to hang up their cleats, but they didn't. Instead of allowing adversity to bury them, they leveraged adversity to elevate their work ethic and they got their ring and their title.

BETHANY HAMILTON

I've always been fascinated by the story of American surfer Bethany Hamilton. Hamilton started surfing when she was just three years old. Five years later, at age eight, she entered her first surfing competition. By the ripe old age of ten, Hamilton secured her first sponsorship deal.[2] I don't know what you were doing when you were ten years old, but I was studying spelling words and meeting animals for the first time. If I'd have known of Bethany Hamilton, I would have thought she was the luckiest girl on earth.

You may have heard this part of Hamilton's story: In 2003, when she was barely a teenager, Hamilton was out surfing one morning along Tunnels Beach on Kauai, Hawaii, with her best friend, Alana. She'd probably done this same routine a thousand times before, but this one would be different. It would alter the trajectory of her life in drastic, permanent ways.

Bethany was lying belly-down on her surfboard, chatting with her bestie with her hand trailing in the water beside her, when a fourteen-foot-long tiger shark attacked her, biting and severing her left arm just below the shoulder.[3] After Bethany was paddleboarded to shore, Alana's father made a tourniquet out of a rash guard to stave off as much of the bleeding as possible.

By the time she was rushed to the hospital, Bethany had lost over half of her body's blood content and was in hypovolemic shock (which basically means very sick due to blood loss). Ironically, Hamilton's dad was already at the hospital getting prepped for knee surgery. She took his place in the operating room.

Years later in an interview with ABC News's Chris Cuomo, Bethany said, "And then, I was holding on to my board, with my thumb, because I probably didn't want to get pulled under. It was like pulling me back and forth, not like pulling me underwater. Just like, you know how you eat a piece of steak?...It was kind of like that. And then it let go. And then went under. Then I looked down at the water, and it was like really red, from all the blood in the water."[4]

Miraculously, Hamilton survived. But if I'd heard her story in the days following the attack, I would have said, "That's horrible. For a shark to attack someone so young, someone with so much potential. Out of anyone in the ocean that day that shark could have attacked, it chose an up-and-coming surfing star. What are the odds? I guess she just had bad luck."

When I think about stories like Bethany's, I realize that bad luck happens and there's not much to be done about it. We're just people living through the human experience, which plays out with both favorable and unfavorable circumstances that are out of our control. So instead of talking about being unlucky or focusing on our odds, we need to shift our attention to the adversity, confront it, and decide how we're going to get beyond it and overcome it.

Just twenty-six days later Hamilton got back on her surfboard. Within two years she had won her first national title competing against able-bodied surfers. "If I thought of myself as disabled I wouldn't be where I am today," she said in a 2020 interview. "I was on a mission to become the best surfer I could be, regardless of what my body looks like."[5]

For obvious reasons, I relate to Bethany's story on a gut level. Though I don't know what life was like before I lost my leg, I imagine I wouldn't be a fraction of the competitor that I am today without the adversity—or "bad luck"—of being disabled. Who knows if I would have ever even become a *runner*? Was the "unluckiest" thing that happened to me (losing my leg) really the unluckiest event of my life? I don't think so.

But that's because I've chosen to not worry about luck and reframe what adversity means in my life. Instead of viewing adversity as a setback that limits me, I choose to view adversity as a setup that will make me better, push me further, and create new opportunities for me if I endure, persevere, and learn. Because if I can endure, persevere, and learn, I create my own odds.

ALIGNMENT

After over a decade as a professional athlete, I still find myself in very "unlucky" or adverse situations. Being a female in sports is tough. At the college level, men's sports have historically gotten more attention and more funding than female sports, especially when it comes to the championship events seen as the school's big moneymakers.

A 2021 report by the law firm of Kaplan Hecker & Fink highlighted the discrimination against female collegiate athletes. It revealed that the NCAA spent $4,285 for men's Division I and national championship participants, excluding basketball. For female participants, the NCAA spent about $1,700 less than that during the season (2018–2019) in question.[6]

The gap is even larger when it comes to single-competitor sports, like wrestling and beach volleyball. The NCAA spends $2,229 more per athlete for the men's championships than for the women's.

The stats don't get better in our postcollege careers. Though the women's US soccer team *did* just settle a gender discrimination suit for $24 million,[7] if you're a girl in professional sports, you're just not going to get the same amount of respect as men. I continue to hope the future of female sports will become more progressive and equal. We put in the same number of hours—if not more. And our working conditions are often way tougher.

So on top of being a professional female athlete, I'm also a para-athlete. And a minority. In other words, adversity is just another day on the track. But in 2017, something incredible happened for me. If I'd ever use the word "luck," I'd use it to describe that season of my career. I experienced luck—or better called *alignment*—on an entirely new level than I ever had before.

In 2017, I broke the world record in the 400 meters. And at some point that season, I also broke the American record in both the 100 and 200 meters. Later that summer in July, I won my first of two global medals in para-athletics track and field by winning bronze in the 100 meters and in the long jump at the World Championships.

It was a season where I felt untouchable.

Everything my team and I did was the right thing. Every button we pushed was the right button. It seemed like every week I got better and better, and my race times started coming down. You couldn't tell us nothing that season. I even walked around with a little swagger. My confidence grew even as the challenges ahead grew.

So I went into the World Championships feeling the same way I did when I took the stage at the middle school spelling bee. Like, *My gosh, this is very doable. I've put in the work. I've done everything within my power to set myself up to be successful. I can win a medal.* And at that time I really thought only the 100 meters medal was on the table. But I was wrong. I ended up winning one in the long jump, too.

Now that isn't to say all of this came easily to me. There's nothing worse than competing in the rain, because it causes so many variables you can't train for. To say it rained during those championships would be like comparing the sun to a desk lamp. There was a torrential downpour. I mean, it was actually hailing during the long jump. I remember being at the start line before my first jump thinking, *This is absolutely insane and crazy.*

Surely, they're going to call it. They didn't. And yet, I was still able to have a performance worthy of a medal.

Was it luck that I'd won? Or was it *alignment?* After all, I had trained for it.

With alignment, you improve your probability. You exit off the highway of mediocrity, and through endurance, perseverance, and humility (an openness to learning new things), you put yourself in the pathway of good outcomes.

The same way difficult times and hard seasons shape and prepare us for the more critical adversities we experience in life, my practices, hours in the gym, mornings and nights spent on the track brought about something I call "alignment."

So 2017 was my year of alignment—when all the work I'd put into training lined up with the right timing and the right team to create the very best chance I had to win.

See, when we put in the hard work, when we do all we can to be diligent and responsible on our end, we increase our chances for success. We create our own odds. It's not enough just to hope your outcomes improve. It's not enough to check all the boxes of the status quo, showing up for school and work and doing the minimum to get by.

No, if you want to advance, you've got to do more and you've got to do it with intentionality. This is how we create the opportunity for "luck" or alignment in our lives.

If I were to have to provide an equation for alignment, these would be the factors:

TRAINING + TIMING + TEAM = ALIGNMENT

Training

People who are able to overcome challenges with grace possess something called a "growth mindset." When confronted with adversity, these people shift their thinking from *Why me?* to *What can this teach me?* It's the difference between being focused on the right now and being able to have a futuristic mindset.

After a particularly tough day on the track, sometimes I'll have to take an ice bath. An ice bath is fifteen minutes of absolute torture. It's so painful. You may have seen these on TV, and they're pretty much what they sound like. You strip naked and climb into a trough-like tub filled with ice-cold water. Ice baths reduce inflammation and improve your body's recovery time by changing the way blood and other fluids flow through your body.

They are also freaking cold and I absolutely hate them. But I know that if I can endure the fifteen minutes of momentary pain, it will pass and I will be better because of it.

Suffering produces strength. And embracing pain in the moment for the glory of tomorrow is a mental toughness skill that every single athlete has to develop within themselves. In practices, in workouts, and in competitions. It's part of our training to compete, and it's just as important as our physical training.

Trust me—I've thrown myself some pretty lavish pity parties over the years. But what might surprise you is that I've never really felt disadvantaged because I am missing my leg.

I've certainly recognized how much better our country and world could do at serving and including people with disabilities, but I don't have a memory of ever having two legs. It's a fact I accept wholly and radically. I've never allowed being disabled to define me, and you don't have to allow any inherent quality about yourself define you, either. But you may have to compensate through training.

Who your family is, what economic status you were born into, how you grew up, or even how well you did in school—none of that is an excuse to forfeit the game. Learn to view these adversities as training opportunities.

How can being raised in a dysfunctional home make me a better parent?

How can being dyslexic make me more intelligent?

How can being hearing impaired make me a better listener?

How can being unpopular make me more empathetic to others?

Look—you have a choice. Adversity can make you bitter or it can make you better. Those who choose to get better are the very ones who appear to be "lucky."

Timing

Timing matters to us only when it's off. Right? We don't even recognize all the moments that have aligned in our favor because they pass us by without calling for our attention. But doesn't it always seem like we're waiting for an unspecified moment in the future for us to be happy, satisfied, or content?

For me, I struggle against living from race to race. I've wished away days, weeks, and months that I'll never get back, holding my breath for my next opportunity to compete.

One thing I've had to work on is understanding that not every single moment can be *my* moment. I've got to take my off seasons with my on ones, and I'll be a whole lot happier if I can find a way to find joy in both.

Whatever you're waiting for right now, whether it be a job, a relationship, an answer to a prayer, a degree, a child, don't allow waiting on that thing or person to rob you of right now. Whatever time it is on whatever day it is that you're reading this? You'll never get the opportunity to live this moment again. See? It's already gone. Time is a nonrenewable resource. We all get an assigned amount and none of us know how much or how little that is.

Learning the discipline of being present in every day and every moment will make you a happier and more peaceful person. It will also give you the space to prepare yourself for when the timing *is* right.

Team

We'll talk about building your team in more detail later, but there is almost nothing more pivotal in your life than the people you choose to spend time with. That goes for friendships, coaches, mentors, even the people you look up to on social media. There's something powerful that happens when our story collides with someone else's, and even more so when we choose to walk through life alongside someone. Just know that there are no static relationship dynamics. The people in your life are either driving you toward your goals or pulling you away from them. Be aware of who you invite onto your team.

I have a team of women around me right now who are actual rock stars. I would be nowhere near where I am personally or professionally without them. How do I know? Because I haven't always made the best choices when it comes to agencies and management. A team who isn't for your best interest is not a good team. And let me add that sometimes you don't even know what your best interests are. Just because someone tells you "no" doesn't mean they shouldn't be on your team.

Now, I know you may not have paid agents and managers, but you do have people who give you advice. Even if they don't directly sit you down and say, "Okay, here's what you should do," you watch how they live their lives and you are influenced by their choices and actions—whether you realize it or not. These are your teammates. Pay attention to your team. Choose them carefully. They're improving your odds or stacking the deck against you.

Training. Timing. Team.

These three factors aligned in 2017 to create an electric atmosphere where I excelled. Was it luck? No, it was something better: alignment that I had trained for. And this alignment isn't something that's unique to Scout Bassett. No, it's something you can work toward, too.

Remember earlier when we said that the "lucky" ones are the ones who choose to reframe adversity as opportunity? They don't compare their lives to others' because they know that like the waves of the ocean, adversity tugs and pushes at us all.

Lucky girls are not kissed by sparkling unicorns before they're born and given a carefree life. In fact, some of the faces you see on TikTok, Instagram, ESPN, and TV are the faces of people who have endured a lot. A *lot*.

Addison Rae, Kim Kardashian, Adele, Lady Gaga, Leonardo DiCaprio, Lizzo, Demi Lovato—all names of celebrities who have openly admitted to struggling with mental health issues they've had to overcome to achieve alignment.

So what adversity is training you right now?

Maybe your parents don't get along.

Maybe you have feelings for someone who doesn't feel the same way.

Maybe you've experienced racism, misogyny, or some other type of discrimination.

Maybe you feel unnoticed and invisible.

Maybe you feel like you should know what you want to do with your life by now, but you don't.

Maybe you've experienced moral failure you don't think you can come back from.

Maybe you feel like you're too much. Maybe you feel like you're not enough.

Maybe you just feel like you don't connect with anyone. You feel lonely. Hopeless.

Honestly, I can relate to every one of those examples of adversity. Of "bad" luck.

But starting today, we're going to stop viewing these circumstances as ones that define us forever. We're instead going to leverage them to ask, "How can this make me better? How can I work on aligning the right areas of my life—training, timing, and team—so that I can grow in confidence and expect good things?"

I want you to face every day with the knowledge I had onstage at the spelling bee and on the track in 2017. If you do the work, good luck will come your way. And really, it won't even be luck at all.

CHAPTER TWO

BEING AN "OTHER"

H ave you ever been asked to check a box on a form in the waiting room of a doctor's office and none of the choices really fit?

"Excuse me, receptionist? Yes, there's no box for 'Chinese-born government orphan and amputee turned adopted American and raised conservative Christian.' What should I mark instead?"

When you're adopted with very little context for your biological family, when you grow up a minority in America, and when you're a person with a disability, *other* becomes a box you get acquainted with.

THE "OTHER"

Growing up and being ethnically Chinese, disabled, and adopted, I can't remember a time when I *didn't* feel like an other. This dynamic was most obvious at school, with my peers, and the sports teams I was on.

I've heard it all. From people commenting on my hair after they've touched it without permission, to people squinting their eyes at me and saying, "How do you see outta those things?" to the insane number of comments I used to get every Halloween when kids would say, "You should be a pirate for Halloween. You've already got a peg leg!"

At the school I went to, I didn't learn anything about Asian Americans, our history, our story, or anything about the suffering that Asians have gone through to be in this country. We also didn't learn about Asian icons or trailblazers. I couldn't even tell you a single person I knew growing up who was an Asian role model. I don't mean just like, in my community. I never even heard about, read about, or saw any Asians on TV. Honestly, it wasn't until I was in college and watched *The Hangover* that I saw an Asian on-screen—Ken Jeong. (Who, by the way, I think is freaking hilarious.)

I remember standing around the field outside of my middle school and a kid randomly pointed to me and said, "You're like, Oriental, aren't you?"

I said, "Do you even know where the Orient is? No. Just say that I'm Asian, *Mike*."

Just kidding. I didn't say that. I wish I'd been that brave and bold back then. It was obvious "Mike" felt compelled to point out the obvious—one was not like the rest and that one was me.

Like I hadn't noticed.

CAN'T RUN, CAN'T HIDE

Manufacturers invest an incredible amount of science and research into making cosmetic legs look as much like your anatomical limb as possible. They try to match the skin tone; they try to match the shape. The foam of the prosthetic is formed over the knee, the foot, and the socket to create a natural-looking limb. You can't even see the actual technology of the limb—the components that help you walk and maintain balance—because you can also wear a cosmetic cover that serves to further disguise the prosthetic.

As hard as you try to make a walking prosthetic look like an anatomical limb or your other leg, it is never one hundred percent dead on. And the minute you spend a day out in the sun, the skin tone paint fades and changes color. It's like walking around with a sunburned leg...indefinitely.

I didn't have the perfect gait—the rhythm and pace you move with when you walk. I remember one Michigan winter I was walking outside the school to go to another part of the building. I slipped on a patch of ice and fell down—which wasn't all that uncommon for me. But a chunk of the foam from my prosthetic leg had escaped both the cosmetic cover *and* my pants and was lying on the ground just beside my foot. I tried quickly to pick it up and shove it in my pocket, but that just made the entire situation more shady and more awkward. The kids who'd stopped to watch the sideshow laughed behind their notebooks.

Technology in prosthetics has come so far since the 1990s and early 2000s, and back when I was in school, prosthetics were not nearly as advanced as they are now. It was impossible to walk like a person with two natural legs. To mask my uneven steps, I would walk slowly. Very, very slowly. Like, what was I thinking? I just envision a twelve-year-old Scout creeping down the hallways of my Christian school with two-toned legs. Talk about sticking out as an "other."

What did all my hiding and masking accomplish for me? Nothing. Everybody knew that I had a prosthetic. When you go to a school with only twelve other kids in your grade, you get to know each other pretty well—for better or for worse. I was known as "that Asian girl with the fake leg." It's almost comical to me now how much I tried to cover up who I was. Like, there was no point. My leg (or lack of leg) was the elephant in every room. The elephant with a limp.

I tried *so hard* to not be different. In fact, for most of my childhood, I resented myself. Isn't that weird? To be mad at yourself and hold a grudge against yourself for things that "yourself" had nothing to do with?

There are things about ourselves that we simply cannot change. For me, I cannot change that I was abandoned. I cannot change that I have only one anatomical leg. I cannot change that I was adopted by a white American family. And I cannot change that I'm Chinese. And yet, so much of my energy was spent trying to do just that.

A GROUP OF "OTHERS"

I get so many messages through social media and in the conversations I have with young women I meet on the road, and do you know what I've found?

You don't have to be a minority to feel like an other.

You don't have to be adopted to feel like an other.

You don't have to be disabled to feel like an other.

While those three attributes definitely don't *help* a person fit in, they're not the only circumstances we experience that make us feel like outsiders. In some ways, in some circles, in some seasons of our lives, we all experience moments when we feel like we don't belong somewhere where we would really like to belong. (Even if we don't want to admit we'd like to belong there.) I think some of us have a difficult time admitting that we want to fit in. Maybe it makes us feel weak or makes us feel like sellouts or followers. But belonging is instinctual. You even see it in animals, who travel in herds. As humans, our instinct to belong is primal—not only fundamental to our happiness and well-being, but also fundamental to our survival. Think about it. Humans are deeply dependent on other humans from the moment we're born. We literally cannot survive on our own. The connections we have to our inner circle aren't a weakness—they're necessary.

I hear people say all the time, "I don't need anybody. I'm better off alone."

Oh really? How would that work out for you as a two-year-old trying to navigate the world? What would you have had for dinner in your Disney princess tent? Marshmallows? Getting older and developing the ability to keep ourselves alive doesn't negate our need to belong.

The concept of needing to belong has roots in social psychology. You guys already know I'm a total nerd, but if science isn't your thing, I'm asking that you stick with me here. I think you can learn some things about yourself that could vastly improve your life. Plus, being well-read and intelligent is attractive. Enough with the "being smart is for losers" trope of every single movie and show we grew up with. Being smart is hot. It's time we all agree on this.

I want to introduce you to three famous experts who have done the reading, research, and studies to prove that human beings are wired for and benefit from "affiliation."

American psychologist Abraham Harold Maslow is best known for his work on a theory of psychological health called Maslow's hierarchy of needs. Basically, Maslow was interested in what makes us happy, healthy, content, and successful individuals.

He lists the first two most basic needs as physiological needs (food, oxygen, water, sleep, etc.) and safety needs (health and security). The third need listed by Maslow is for love and belonging.

Maslow defined belongingness as referring "to a human emotional need for interpersonal relationships, affiliating, connectedness, and being part of a group. Examples of belongingness needs include friendship, intimacy, trust, and acceptance, receiving and giving affection, and love."[1] According to Maslow, a failure to meet "the love needs" that include striving for "love and affection and belongingness" results in a deficient mental and behavioral state for all humans. All of them. All of *us*.

You'd probably admit your need to be loved way quicker than your need to belong. Again, because as a society, we've got a cynical, sort of warped view of needing others. But Maslow placed needing love and needing to belong on the very same level, even above our need to feel respected, accomplished, and purposeful.

In 1995, two professors of psychology by the names of Roy Baumeister and Mark Leary published the findings of a study they'd conducted on the need to belong as a basic human motivation. According to their research, fulfilling the need to belong requires two steps. First, people need to have relatively frequent, positive interactions with at least a few other people. Second, these interactions must take place within a framework of long-lasting affective concern for each other's welfare.[2]

Meeting one or the other of these criteria alone is not sufficient to fulfill the need: Positive interactions outside of long-lasting relationships will not be completely satisfying and neither will long-term relationships that lack regular contact. In other words, we need people who care about us—and vice versa—in our everyday lives.

Like Maslow, Baumeister and Leary's research didn't illustrate belonging as just a desire, but as a basic human need. Failure to satisfy this need should be met with serious concern and will likely result in negative long-term consequences.

It's important to understand that our struggle and anguish and embarrassment and pain and anger from feeling like an "other" is directly connected to our need to belong. You're not weak for wanting to belong. You're not a sellout. You're not a follower. You're a human.

Needing to belong doesn't mean you want to be the "it" girl at your school, at your job, or in your friend group. Although, that might not suck. You'd still experience bouts of "otherness" because you'd still be a person surfing those waves of adversity. Wanting to belong runs so much deeper than a vain drive for social interaction with visible people. It's about forming a connection over time with people who really care about you, who you really care about too. And when the world, culture, or even our own insecurities tell us we're an "other" who won't ever fit in anywhere, it's a pretty miserable feeling. Our need for belonging is jeopardized, and innately, we panic.

Something I've learned about human nature is that we like to assign titles to other people. We like to categorize. Put things, people, and places into nice little boxes that give us context for our experiences. Take Mike at my middle school, for example. Constantly tugging his eyes to mimic my slanted features or pointing out that I'm "Oriental." Mike needed to label me to make himself feel more at ease. To make Mike feel more in control. This is an obvious correlation, but when we're familiar with something, we feel we have power over it. If you've ridden a bike a thousand times, you have no problem hopping on a bike without another thought. We excel in scenarios where we can easily contextualize our environment, but to Mike, preteen Scout made absolutely no sense.

It's pretty easy to automatically hate the Mikes of the world, but honestly, we're all this way. Maybe we all don't react with microaggressions, but we seek to qualify and quantify one another.

NOT ASIAN ENOUGH

I could count on one hand the number of minority residents of my hometown. Two of them went to my school, but we weren't really friends. Believe it or not, we don't "all know each other" and we aren't "all related" or something.

So when I went to college at UCLA, I was stoked to meet other people who looked like I did—at least in ethnicity. They call UCLA the "University of Caucasians Lost Among Asians." The racial demographics are flipped from most big universities, with Asians being the largest population on campus. When I met my dormmate my first year, I was convinced we were about to be lifelong friends. She was second-generation Chinese American. Her parents actually immigrated to the United States before she was born.

But it didn't take very long for me to realize that my dreams of late-night chats and daily runs to the dining hall were *not* in our future. To her, I was also an other.

"What is that?" I asked her as she unpacked.

She looked at me like I must be joking, but then she saw that I wasn't. "It's a rice cooker, Scout. What Chinese person doesn't own a rice cooker?"

When she looked at me, she saw how very Chinese I was. But when she talked to me, she saw how very Chinese I wasn't. I was juggling so many identities, I didn't even know how to classify "what" I was.

Eventually, my dormmate couldn't take the guessing game anymore. "Scout," she said after declining yet another invitation to hang out, "you're just not authentic enough for me."

What she meant was I just wasn't *Asian* enough for her.

A lot of Asian kids are raised with Asian family members and parents who all speak their native language at home. By the time I got to college, I hadn't spoken Chinese in over a decade. I lost my use of the language a few years after being brought to the United States. I was raised by a white family. We didn't celebrate any Chinese holidays or observe any Asian traditions or customs. For my dormmate, I was too culturally white to be Asian.

Not white enough to be white, mind you.

But not Asian enough to be Asian.

"Hapa" is a Hawaiian word that means "part." It has spread beyond the islands and into slang to describe someone who is half Asian and half something else. Even though my ethnicity is fully Asian, I always felt hapa, or half. Never fully being enough of anything to belong.

By high school I had made a few white friends at my private Christian academy. The older we got, the more we talked about our future hopes and dreams. This particular community was very conservative and traditional. While pretty much everyone I graduated with pursued higher education, for the most part, they planned to go to community college close to home, get married, have babies, and do the family thing as quickly as possible.

Cue Scout's otherness.

I remember being in the girls' locker room and it sort of dawned on me that I had literally nothing in common with anyone else around me. "I'm not going to do any of that," I said. "I want to move out to the West Coast and get a job in social media or in marketing. I want to live before I settle down."

I might as well have announced my plans to become an assassin. Everyone's ponytail flipped my way as they stared at me like I'd just grown a leg instead of having a missing one.

In my hometown, you didn't leave. It's a generational area where you buy your grandparents' property to fix up after college because they've passed it on and it's got to stay in the family.

While I think those choices are perfectly acceptable and even beautiful, they weren't the choices for me.

I'd always felt this way. I remember playing youth soccer as a *little* kid and someone on my team asking me what I wanted to do when I got older. "I don't know what I want to do yet," I said, "but I'm not going to do anything that everybody else here does."

I didn't mean it as a slap in the face to anyone. It was just like, *I want to get out of here. I want to see the world. I want to do something new and exciting.* I knew people thought I was crazy. I even had a teacher tell me that I needed to know my limits. Like, "Scale back those dreams, Scout. We can't have you emphasizing your otherness by wanting more for your life."

I didn't have specific ideas of what my future was going to look like. But being a dreamer, I announced my plans to get out of Michigan just as soon as I was able to pretty much anyone who asked…or didn't ask. I was a dreamer. Which drew plenty of scoffing and laughter from my peers. While it was hard to hear their reactions to my "escape plan," it honestly didn't bother me very much. Somehow, I knew at that young age they wouldn't understand.

My story, my path was different because I was different. But I didn't want my life to look like theirs in the future, so why had I been so concerned with why my life didn't look like theirs *now*? I was beginning to see that being set apart from the herd wasn't such a bad thing after all.

During a conference with my parents, my teacher was sure to point out my "rebellion."

"Scout talks a *lot* about a big future, away from here," she said in a grave tone. "I've spoken with her about this, but she just keeps on and on." You'd have thought I'd gotten caught smoking in the bathroom.

I learned two things from this teacher:

1. Nontraditional paths make some people uncomfortable.
2. Being different makes you stand out. (But standing out is a good thing.)

When you share your dreams with some people—and especially if your dreams are unconventional—their responses will likely be something like this: "That will never happen. You can't do it. And you're bad/wrong/stupid for wanting those things." If you've had someone say any variation of those things to you after sharing your dreams with them, I want you to take the words they said to you, mentally roll them up like a wad of trash, and throw them away in the dark recesses of your mind. Their response had way more to do with their lives than yours.

As an adult looking back, I actually feel bad for that teacher. There was a real hardness to her she directed at all of her students that didn't add up. It was obvious something in her background or in her current situation had wounded her, and that wound had definitely not healed.

But more importantly, what I learned from this experience with my teacher is that I stood out. That was obvious. That part wasn't exactly news. I mean, I was the adopted Asian girl with one leg. But as I've gotten older, I've realized that standing out doesn't have to be a bad thing. In fact, at some point, you're going to *want* to stand out. You're going to want to be seen, noticed, and acknowledged. And if you're different—if you're an other—you can leverage what makes you different to elevate your platform and your purpose.

YOUR "OTHER" GIFT

I love Steve Harvey. If you don't know who that is, search him online. He's hilarious. Steve is a TV host, actor, writer, producer, and comedian. I don't watch a lot of television, but I do see his videos online and I always stop to hear what he's saying. The man has some pretty incredible stories, and I remember one he shared that stuck with me.

Steve was talking about the things that made him an other. Things like having a stutter that was so severe, he couldn't talk unless he was at home. He shared about struggling in school and eventually failing out. He talked about his problems in relationships, being on his third marriage at the time. He'd even lived in his car for *three years*. Steve for sure knew what it felt like to be an other. And here's what he said about his experience:

[God] turned me into something I never saw, I ain't think I'd ever be this. People come to me from everywhere, I meet with kings and queens. I was in Botswana with the president and the first lady of Botswana. Then I met the crown prince of Abu Dhabi. He came out of his chair at the race to come meet me. You know why he came to meet me? Just simply because of my gift. I make people laugh. It put me in the presence of great men. That's what my gift has done for me. That's what your gift will do for you.[3]

See, Steve saw his *otherness* the same way I slowly started to see my own. As a *gift*. As the thing that makes us *us*. Your otherness holds a mirror to your unique wiring. Maybe you're into comics and anime and your purpose is to be an insanely talented graphic artist. Or maybe you're into books like I was. You read voraciously because books are your escape. You could be the next J. K. Rowling. Maybe you're into cars, tattoos, vampires, lacrosse, chess, cats, whatever. Who you are sets you apart and can eventually become your superpower...if you let it.

I also know there are people reading this who aren't sure how their otherness could ever possibly lead to something good or productive. Don't forget—I didn't start running until I was a teenager. My otherness was just that—otherness—for most of my childhood and adolescence. It's okay not to know exactly how your life is going to play out. In fact, it's normal. Maybe right now your otherness just feels like otherness—your insurmountable obstacle to fitting in.

Give it time. Give yourself time. Give God time to slowly reveal His plan for you. That was the turning point for me.

Growing up in a very conservative Christian home, I often found it difficult to connect to a God who was all about restrictions and rules. But remember what I said about adults not always being right? Well, I learned in time I had to define what a relationship with God meant to me. To Scout Bassett. Who was God in my life?

If I believed I was intentionally created, surely there had to be a reason—better than that—a *purpose* for my otherness. Look, I'm not going to tell you what to believe. I don't know where you stand on faith and God and church, or whether or not your spiritual life is something that's important to you. But I can tell you with certainty that my personal faith and spiritual journey have been an anchor to me throughout my life. It's not something you can rely on someone else for. It's got to be something you figure out for yourself—what it means to you, if anything.

If you're not sure what you believe, I encourage you to have an open mind as we read together. Actually, even if you are sure what you believe. Being open to learning new or different ways of thinking is the only way to grow as a person.

When I was nine years old, I remember being at a park near my house. I always had a lot of energy, and my parents didn't know what to do with me. So I played outside a *lot*. There was a group of kids I stopped to watch. They were climbing up the slide and then sliding back down on their stomachs. It looked fun.

One of the little girls said to the other, "Does she want to play?"

The girl studied me. I was maybe two feet away from them. The silence expanded awkwardly between us. "She can't play," she finally said, pointing to my leg. "She doesn't have enough legs."

I was very small for my age, so these kids were maybe five years old. I can almost laugh about it now, but in the moment, I was devastated. English was still very new to me, but I knew exactly what they meant: No Others Allowed.

Instinctively, I felt that something was terribly wrong, but I also somehow knew this experience would not be the last one of its kind. I was right. And though those moments of exclusion have all been crushing at a first glance, they are priceless when I look back at them. I would not be who I am today, I would not know what I know today, I would not be capable of accomplishing what I've accomplished today without being an other. Being an other doesn't have to make you a victim. Being an other could be your path to victory.

People laughed at my otherness. They definitely scoffed at my dreams. I'm sure they thought, *Scout, you can't even jump rope. How are you going to travel the world?* But I just knew I would. What's made me different has become my opportunity. My chance. My pass. My otherness has given me the life I dreamed of.

If God didn't want me to be Chinese, I wouldn't be Chinese. If God didn't want me to have a prosthetic, I would have two legs. At some point, we have to trust that the Creator knows more than us—knows better than us. I had to come to the point where I asked, "What good can possibly come from this? What is the purpose that God has in this? Because this can't be an accident."

Around high school, I started to have a mind shift when I started running. For the first time I experienced feelings of freedom, which helped me develop more confidence. Don't allow your otherness to lead you to embrace a victim mentality. Victims are always victims—never the winners.

Maybe all us others need is a little faith. Faith in ourselves, faith in God's plan.

Being an other is a lonely place to be. I get that. And I'm not going to pretend that it always feels good and that you should ignore those feelings of isolation. What I'd love to be true for you is that you learn to shift your perspective, just a little bit at first. If there's something different about you, why not consider how your differences make you a person with a unique perspective? Someone who has something different to say? Who has new ideas?

You also have the ability to help *other* others. You have stories and experiences they can relate to. Whether you have a disability, are a minority, have a different religion, or you're a big, bold dreamer. Whatever qualities that separate you from "the crowd," I hope you try to use them for good. That's what I'm trying to do.

If you're reading this right now and you feel like an "other," here's what I'd say to you: Do not hide. Please, don't hide. Don't mask who you are. Don't be ashamed or embarrassed. If you're lucky enough to be an other, that's important. It's special because it means you're different. You're not like other people, but that comes with a plan, a purpose, and a path. Your path's not going to look like everybody else's, but aren't you glad? You have something no one else does. You're an other. And that's a box anyone should be proud to check.

CHAPTER THREE

UNMET EXPECTATIONS

I was recently at dinner with friends at our favorite Mexican spot. I try to eat really healthy, but you know your girl needs some queso and guac every now and then. My toxic trait is that I will absolutely get full on chips and salsa before the food arrives and that night was no different.

Our server, Daniel, took everyone's order, and when he came to my friend Jess, she said, "I'll have grilled chicken tacos. And please make sure they don't come in contact with the shrimp tacos, because I have a severe shellfish allergy."

I don't have a huge group of friends, but the ones I do have I love deeply. When it comes to friendships, quality over quantity all day long.

Anyway, everyone's food arrived and we cleared away the chips and salsa to make room for our fajitas, tacos, and quesadillas. I may be a petite girl, but I have an appetite. We were all taking our first bites—you know, the best bite, the one where there are seconds of nothing but chewing and smacking—when my girlfriend Jess yelped.

"No!" she said. "No, no, no!"

She grabbed her water and filled her mouth with it, swished it around, then spit it out. She did this a few times before she got out the words "It's shellfish."

We all swung into action.

"Where's her EpiPen?" somebody yelled.

Chairs and napkins went flying. Plates smashed to the ground. Everybody around us stood up and a few even tried to help.

"Don't...have it...tonight," Jess managed. Her face was already swelling and there were raised blotches of red along her chest and jaw.

By the time the ambulance showed up, Jess was taking deep gasps of air, struggling for breaths as her throat continued to swell closed. Thankfully, Jess was all right, but she did spend a night in the hospital to be monitored.

This is a true story, by the way. And if you're reading this, Daniel, I'd like to speak to your manager.

I'm not sure how this mix-up happened. He probably heard

"Anything but shrimp," and the word "shrimp" stuck. I don't think he was intentionally trying to hurt my friend. I mean, he *better* not have been. Even though I'm sure it was an accident, you can believe I was pissed.

It would be a remarkable understatement to say that the night did not go as expected. For anyone.

When you expect to bite into a chicken taco and it's actually a taco that could kill you, you're caught off guard. You're angry. You're scared. You're scattered. Your expectations have gone unmet.

Unmet expectations hurt. It's like losing something you never even had.

We've all got expectations. We may not realize it until they're *not* met, but they're there. In his book *The Expectation Effect*, David Robson says that "our expectations are like the air we breathe—they accompany us everywhere, yet we are rarely conscious of their presence."[1]

We expect the sun to rise. We expect the seasons to change. We expect to grow up, go to school, graduate college, get a good job, find someone to love, get married, have a family, and retire to some tropical destination. Obviously, these aren't everyone's expectations. They certainly weren't mine for myself. But you get the idea. We have these subtle plans about what should and will happen in our lives.

But what happens when our expectations go unmet? When we take a bite out of a shrimp taco when we're expecting chicken?

EXPECTATIONS ON OURSELVES

In 2012, I went out to the trials for the 2012 Paralympic team to compete in London. I had been in the sport for only about two years leading up to those trials. I was nervous, but I wanted to give it a shot and see how I measured up against the other girls in my events. I knew I wasn't going to place first, but I couldn't help but be excited to see where I fell in the pack. At the end of the last race, I looked at the times, calculating how I lined up against the others, and...

I came in last place. In both the 100 and 200 meters.

Now, I knew it would be a long shot for me to qualify for the Games, and I didn't expect a trophy, but I certainly expected better. To not even be close to the *middle* of the field felt disappointing and humiliating. I had no idea I was that far behind the other female athletes I was racing against. Not only was I obviously not in a position to make the team, but I remember the *fear* I felt about how far I had to go, how far away I was from the rest of the girls. We weren't even in the same realm.

Sometimes when we expect something from ourselves and we don't quite hit the mark, it can reinforce preexisting negative thoughts and feelings we have about ourselves. I thought, *I'll never be a competitor. I never got to compete much as a kid, so I haven't had the same training that these girls have had. I should just give up. I'll never get to where they are.*

But looking back, I sort of want to smack myself upside the

head. I'd been training for two years. *Two.* When I graduated from college, I didn't go straight to the sport. I worked in corporate America. I wore dresses, went to meetings, and sold medical devices. Sure, I'd run, but the sport wasn't my job. I trained when I could, but it wasn't what I did for a living. Most of the girls at the trials were lifers. They had coaches to push and teach them and sponsorships that allowed them to work at running full time. I should have just been proud to show up at the starting line.

But I've always been this way with myself—I've always expected a lot. Sometimes too much. I have always carried the weight of representing marginalized people—those with disabilities, women, Asians.

For example, I never saw people with disabilities in mainstream media. Which is ironic, since 26 percent of Americans (one in four) have some sort of disability.[2] Only 3.1 percent of television shows feature people with disabilities, and that number is even lower for kids' shows—less than 1 percent.[3]

Despite these stats, you didn't see people with disabilities in entertainment or in the media. And frankly, I didn't see a lot of Asian people doing those things, either. It's not like there were a lot of portrayals of Asians in movies or on TV shows. You didn't see them on covers of magazines or books. I didn't know how I was going to change that, but I had dreams that it was possible. I just expected that I would do something great.

Having expectations for yourself is healthy. You should expect yourself to work hard. To be honest. To be a good listener and a good friend. You should expect yourself to give maximum effort in all you do. But if you're holding yourself to impossible standards, like I was at the 2012 trials, you're setting yourself up for disappointment.

How do you know the difference between healthy expectations and unhealthy expectations for yourself? Here are a few signs you may be expecting too much from yourself:

1. **You find yourself people-pleasing.** I am so guilty of this one. If a server brings me the wrong order, I'd rather choke down sushi than ask for the steak I actually ordered. A people pleaser is someone whose reflex response is "I'm sorry!" Pleasers expect themselves to make everyone around them happy at all times. They find it impossible to say no, even when they really want and need to. If you have sent the "Are you mad at me?" text more than a couple of times…you might be a people pleaser.

2. **You are a perfectionist who never feels good enough.** Perfectionists crave approval, but constructive criticism makes them highly defensive. Perfectionists don't just think that their way is the best way—they think it's the only way. Perfectionists may come off as confident, but they're hypercritical of themselves and never feel satisfied, content, or even proud.

3. **You constantly compare yourself to others.** It's natural to measure yourself against someone else. That's my world—comparing times, technique, and performance. But people who constantly compare themselves to others because they have unhealthy self-expectations usually come off as "one-uppers." If you have something new, they have something newer. If you have something big, they have something bigger. If you have something great, they have something greater. Or it's someone who can't ever be happy with what they have.

If any of those describe you, you may have unhealthy self-expectations. I think we can all enter this space if we're not careful. When you feel yourself people-pleasing, being a perfectionist, or comparing yourself to others, pause. Ask yourself, "What unrealistic expectation am I placing on myself right now?" Adjust. And move on. Because your expectations aren't the only ones you're going to contend with. You'll also be up against the expectations of others.

EXPECTATIONS OF OTHERS

As if managing our *own* expectations wasn't challenging enough, we also have to contend with the expectations of others. Which is a topic I happen to be an expert on.

A lot of people who are non-Asian look at Asians as the "model minority." If there is a model minority in this country, it's Asian people. We're rule followers. We're smart. We're well educated and hardworking. We're submissive and we do not create waves. That's the Asian stereotype and, well, stereotypes exist for a reason. And while those are certainly not bad characteristics to be known for, for me, those expectations have been almost traumatizing to live up to. Because if you don't meet those expectations, you feel like a failure. Not just in general, but like, a failure to your heritage.

I'll give you an example of this. When I went to UCLA, I started out as a biochemistry major. So, of course, everyone on campus is like, "That makes sense. You're Asian." It was almost as if people were applauding me for staying in my racial lane. But then in my sophomore year, I realized I hated biochemistry. It was boring. It didn't excite me. Sure, I was good at it. But that didn't mean I had to keep doing it if I didn't enjoy it.

So I switched to the humanities school—the polar opposite end of the field-of-studies spectrum. I started taking classes like psychology, sociology, anthropology—courses that studied people and culture. I was fascinated. I knew that's where I wanted to be. All of my friends were so confused. I remember one friend said, "But Scout, I thought you wanted to be really successful?"

After college I did go on to work for a medical device company. I don't know why—actually, I do. It was what was expected of me! I hated it. I knew I wasn't doing what I was created to do when I started to dread going into work every day. The only time I felt like Scout Bassett was when I was running. So I took a huge risk and walked away from a successful career to do sports full time. You want to talk about creating waves! You would have thought I told people I had decided to occupy Mars.

Everyone was disappointed in me. Everyone. Friends, family, my colleagues at work. My parents were the most upset. My dad said, "You've gone to UCLA. You've gotten this incredible education. You're doing something important. Why would you give that up?"

One of my closest friends is second-generation Chinese. She was in med school at the time. Her parents were so proud of her, and I remember her calling me and saying, "Scout. This is crazy. What are you doing?"

"I'm not sure," I said. "But I'm not staying miserable just because other people think I should be doing something different."

Selling medical devices wasn't my idea of a limitless future. In fact, it felt like a stifling, miserable grind of a future. My choice was a shocking move for a number of reasons, but the one I heard the most was that Asian people don't do these things. Like, Scout. Who do you think you are? Asians don't switch out of biochem. Asians don't get degrees in sociology and anthropology. And Asians definitely don't become professional athletes.

It felt like I was entering all these spaces I didn't belong in because of other people's expectations.

Another way I haven't met the expectation of being the "model minority" Asian is that I care about and speak on political issues—especially in recent years. I've been more outspoken on social issues and human rights issues. And I know that's ruffled a lot of feathers. Because, again, Asian people are not outspoken. Both Asians and non-Asians alike have responded with surprise. "Oh, you have something to say? We didn't know you had opinions." They don't say those things verbatim, but that's what's implied in their responses. Because in our culture, you just don't talk about those things.

Then there are the expectations around my disability. I could write an entire book on these. On one hand, the expectations for anyone with a disability are generally low. If you're not able-bodied, you're not respected as someone who is. For example, people are taken back when they learn I live alone.

This all leads to the conflicting expectations I've experienced as a disabled Asian. You should be smart because you're Asian. Okay. Check that box. I had something like a 4.6 GPA. I got into every school I applied to, including Ivy Leagues. That made sense. But then I'm also disabled. Which led people to assume that even though I am intelligent, I probably wouldn't accomplish very much because I'm also disabled.

Let me give you an example. Every season of every school year from second grade through high school, I'd sign up to play a sport. And every season it would end up the same. I'd sign up, be on the team, but then have to sit on the sidelines and watch as everyone else played. It felt like I was a mascot, not a team member. No one was willing to give me a chance to compete.

When I was in eighth grade, I played on our high school's JV softball team. And my coach didn't let me participate in one single game. Not one game, inning, or play. I sat in the dugout the entire season. It felt like there was no reason for me to not get a shot. I assume I didn't play because I was disabled, which felt gross and unfair. So I decided to tell my coach what's up.

I laugh about this now, but I was very serious when I unclicked my binder and removed a single sheet of loose-leaf paper. I wrote the coach this superlong letter telling her I was quitting, and I did *not* appreciate how she and the other girls on the team were treating me or excluding me. I told her how disappointed I was in her leadership, or lack thereof. I'm not always that expressive with my emotions, but I had been silent too long. There was a time or two I even cried about not getting to play. I'm not a person who cries. But I'd bottled up years' worth of frustrations. And they all spewed out across the page of that paper. I filled up every single line!

I remember folding up the paper into three crisp folds and putting it in one of those letter-size envelopes and carefully writing her name on the front of it before tucking it into my backpack. I was armed. I had it all planned out. I would make this dramatic entrance into practice and hand the letter over. I'd have coach read it out loud so everyone could hear just how terrible of a person and coach she was. There'd be some sort of ballad playing in the background. Maybe a tear on her cheek. Realizing the error of their ways, the team would actually rally to my defense, encircling me in a huddle before putting me on their shoulders and chanting my name.

That would show the coach.

The next morning I woke up and immediately threw away the letter. The last thing I wanted was to come off sounding childish and ridiculous. And that letter, at best, was both. Quitting wasn't the best way to communicate the point that I'm a player capable of blowing away the coach's expectations. If anything, it would affirm her suspicions that I never measured up all along. Besides, I've learned that if you surrender and quit under the weight of someone else's expectations (or lack of expectations), you give away your power. And that's what expectations are about—power and control. I don't know about you, but I want to be in control of my own life. Of who I become. I don't want to be led around by the leash of what or who someone else thinks I should be.

There's a journalist, author, TV host, basically all-around-badass lady I really admire named Elaine Welteroth. At just thirty years old, Elaine was named editor in chief of *Teen Vogue*, making her both the youngest and second person of color to hold the role. There's a book by Elaine that is a must-read: *More Than Enough: Claiming Space for Who You Are (No Matter What They Say)*. The entire book is gold, but one thing Elaine said in it gets at the heart of how we should view the expectations of others—whether you're Asian, disabled, marginalized, or simply just a woman in America. And it's this: "When you exist in spaces that weren't built for you, remember sometimes that just being you is the revolution. You have done enough. You are enough. You were born enough. The world is waiting on you."[4]

If I'd let the expectations of others dictate my choices in life, I wouldn't be me. I'd have a different degree, a different career, a different group of friends, a different set of goals, and a very, very different life. I would never have become a professional athlete, and I definitely wouldn't have Paralympic medals hanging in my trophy case. I've spent most of my life trying to be me *despite* the expectations of others. I haven't always been as tough as I've wanted to be, but as I've gotten older and grown more comfortable in my own skin, choosing what works for me has become easier and easier.

Sometimes, just being *you* is the most courageous, most bold, most revolutionary act you can do in this life.

So…who are *you*? Without the unhealthy expectations you have for yourself? Without the expectations society has for you? Who are *you*?

Ask yourself the following questions:
1. What kind of music do I like?
2. What do I like to do in my downtime?
3. What shows do I like to binge?
4. What is my dream job?

5. Where would I like to travel?
6. What makes me laugh?
7. What makes me cry?
8. How do I like to dress?
9. What's my favorite place to eat?
10. Who do I admire?

Were you able to answer those questions without thinking about what other people would think? And even if you answered them honestly, would you have the boldness to live out your answers? I hope so. If the answer is yes, then you're being *you* and that's something to be proud of. But if your responses or your actions are influenced by what someone else expects, it's time to set yourself free! If you're living based off someone else's expectations, you may not even know what you really want. You're not realizing how completely freaking awesome *you* are.

And hear me when I say this: The world needs who you are. I believe we were all created with a highly specialized purpose. There's a you-shaped hole in the story of life. I know that sounds cheesy. But something being cheesy doesn't make it untrue.

You've got to make the decision for yourself to not live by culture's expectations, because if you do live by those expectations, you're going to end up chasing your tail around and around and around.

Remember what I said about the conflicting messages I got

from society? That I should be smart because I'm Asian, but not accomplish much because I'm disabled? I'm sure you've experienced your own version of this. Because that's sort of society's deal, right? Conflicting messages of what and who they expect us to be.

As women, they want us to be…

smart, but not a know-it-all

sexy, but not slutty

curvy, but not fat

thin, but not skinny

fit, but not masculine

honest, but not direct.

The pendulum of society is not one I'd ever attach myself to, because you never know when it's going to swing in the other direction, throwing you right off. That's one of the many reasons you can't allow expectations to define you.

Expectations come in layers, don't they? We have them for ourselves, other people have them for us. And, hey, we have them for other people too. Let's be honest. Regardless of the direction an expectation comes from, know this: Expectations *always* limit futures. Always. Expectations tell you how much you can grow, how far you can reach, and how much you can achieve.

The only way to avoid being misled by expectations is to know who you are and to choose that person every single day, over and over again. Give her a shot at a limitless future. She's worth it.

CHAPTER FOUR

LONELINESS

I'm going to talk to you about someone I've only recently been able to open up about. And even now, as I write this, I cry when I think of her. It's emotional for me. Extremely difficult.

Let's call her Hope. Because to me, that's what she was. I can't even remember her real name, but that doesn't make her any less significant in the story of my life.

Hope was another kid who was in the orphanage with me in Nanjing, China. There's a video montage my parents made of their adoption of me, and in it is a photo of me that my parents received of me before they came to get me. I'm sitting at a table with a little girl sitting beside me—Hope. In the photo she leans toward me, almost protectively, her head hovering just over mine like two siblings at the dinner table.

Hope had to be about three years older than me in the photo, dangerously close to the dreaded age of ten. At the orphanage at that time, they had a policy where at ten years old, you had to leave. You were kicked out. It's not really clear what exactly happened to these kids, but my assumption based on what I know now is that they all became homeless. I don't know if they were put in factories to work or were just left out in the streets, but what I do know is that you couldn't stay at the orphanage after you turned ten.

Hope was not disabled. She was just a girl. That's probably why she was in the orphanage—because of China's one-child policy. What's the one-child policy? You're not going to believe this is real life, but in the 1980s, China instituted a one-child per family policy nationwide. The program was intended to curb overcrowding in China, but it ended up having some pretty horrific consequences—forced abortions and sterilizations among them.

But one of the most heartbreaking results was that families who preferred boys (which was basically every family) would cast aside firstborn daughters or firstborns with disabilities. And when I say cast aside, I mean treated like trash—left in the streets, given away, or put in orphanages. Which is probably why Hope was with me in Nanjing.

Hope was my sister. Not biologically, of course, but in every other way that matters. I needed Hope. I had an obvious disability, burns up and down my legs, and up until I was five or six, I didn't even have a walking prosthetic. I would just scoot around on my bum and hands to get around. Hope saw that. She noticed, and she did something about it.

Hope helped me do just about everything. She took me to the bathroom; she would help me get into bed—a bed we shared for as long as I can remember during my stay at the orphanage. There were many times during the day while we were doing chores when Hope would pick me up and carry me just so I could keep up.

Hope made sure I got my bowl of rice, when it was available for us. I weighed twenty-two pounds when I was adopted, but I don't know I would have even weighed that much had it not been for Hope. In fact, I'm confident I would not have lived through my stay in Nanjing without her. She was my legs, but more than that, she was my protector. My companion. My only friend. Hope kept me going—not just physically, but emotionally. But it was like, as long as I had *her*—as long as I had Hope—I had something to look forward to. With Hope, I was able to survive.

One morning I woke up and Hope wasn't in the bed. I looked around.

"Where's Hope?" I asked a caretaker who passed. She didn't answer.

I scooted from the bed clumsily, not accustomed to doing

so without Hope's help, and went to look in the bathroom. It wasn't like her to leave me on my own. I knew something was terribly wrong.

"Hope?" I called. My voice echoed off the walls and urine-stained floors. No answer. The panic grew.

I moved as quickly as I could, looking for Hope everywhere she might be. But she wasn't there. Hope was gone. I asked everyone—"Where is Hope?"—but no one would answer me. I don't know if it was their policy to not discuss the aged-out orphans, or if they couldn't bear to twist the knife of truth. But no one ever told me what had happened to Hope. To this day—I still don't know.

It took me weeks to admit she wasn't coming back. It's not like they made some grand announcement that when you turn ten, you're out. But I knew all along somewhere in the corners of my heart, in the place where you tuck away things you don't want to acknowledge—Hope was never coming back.

I was seven at the time, and I'd known pain and grief on a grand scale. We were orphans at a state-run facility in a country that viewed children as national burdens. It wasn't like our lives as children were full of Saturday morning cartoons and trips to the zoo. But nothing felt as crushing as losing Hope. The only way I can describe the loneliness that followed was that it was like a death. I remember thinking, *I'm dying. This is what it feels like to die.* But, cruelly, the world kept spinning and the sun kept on rising and setting—all without Hope.

In an environment where so few people know what you're going through, where the day-to-day trauma and abuse and unspeakable experiences knit you and friends together closer than family, my bond with Hope was like glue. When she was ripped away from me, it splintered me, taking a part of me with her.

My relationship with Hope is difficult to verbalize to the average person. When you live in an orphanage and there's already so much loss and rejection, you can't avoid experiencing abandonment issues. Then, when you find a connection with someone who cares about you, and you care about them, you feel this magnetic, almost desperate attachment to that person. I don't think this is unique to orphans, but I do think it's felt more strongly by those who don't have a family.

I just *knew* I'd never be able to love someone again after losing Hope. It took me a really long time to get past that loss. It's difficult to even write about now. I wonder where she is. If she made it. If, by some miracle, it wasn't the ten-year-old policy that took Hope away and maybe she was adopted. If anyone deserved it, it was Hope. Looking back, I sometimes wonder if she was an actual angel. I *do* believe she was sent by God to keep me safe. But there's no question there was an empathy and compassion in Hope that was atypical for any kid or adult in my life at the time or even that I've encountered since.

You've got to think about just how selfless Hope's friendship was. While it wasn't unheard of to have a disability in our orphanage, it also wasn't all that common. Most kids were there because of the one-child policy. So for Hope to have seen me struggle and to have entered into that struggle with me, she must have been incredibly courageous and loving. Brave, too. She didn't win any social points for being my best friend.

I don't have a single bad memory of Hope. Not one. We never fought or even disagreed, really. When you're trying to stay alive, there are very few things that are valuable enough to argue about. But Hope never did me wrong. She never belittled me or grew frustrated or impatient with my immobility.

I think that's part of why her absence hit so hard. I wasn't exactly integrated or included with the other kids all that often. But with Hope, I felt like I had a safe place—a home. Hope was my place of acceptance. Without her, I didn't know how to belong. I didn't know how to live. I wish I could sit across a table from Hope right now. I'd tell her thank you. I'd tell her I love her, even today. And I'd tell her that she saved my life. I think she'd be proud of me—like any older sister would be.

The obvious truth is that loneliness is a natural byproduct of life in an orphanage. But what I've learned since is that loneliness is a natural byproduct of life...period. I assumed that being adopted would cure the ache in my chest that I identified as loneliness, but I've felt lonely on varying levels during almost every season of my life since. While nothing compares to losing Hope, coming to America was certainly *not* the cure for loneliness.

FAMILY MATTERS

Aside from friendships, the most pivotal relationships in our lives are the relationships we have with our families. I don't talk about my family publicly very often out of respect for them and their individual journeys, but it's impossible to tell my story without also talking about my family. What I share next is based on my limited perspective, so read knowing that I may not have all the facts and details. I'm just speaking based on my own experience.

When people hear I was adopted at eight years old, they always say, "Wow! That's incredible! Your parents must be amazing people. You are so lucky, Scout."

I agree with so much of that sentiment, but like most situations, my family life wasn't what most people perceive it to have been.

I was adopted at an older age than when most kids are adopted—when they're babies, and when they don't know anything else. I knew a life before I came here, and even though it wasn't a great life, being ripped from that situation and thrust into an entirely new and complicated world was very traumatizing for me. It didn't feel like a positive thing for a very long time. I felt I was stripped of my language, my culture, and the identity of who I was. I felt I was asked to become someone very different, and was given no other choice but to take on this new life. Scout Bassett was hoisted onto my frail shoulders.

I didn't have the most ideal family situation, even after I was adopted. I felt there was a lot of instability in our family—a lot of strife and tension. I didn't have a foundation of family support and structure pushing me or encouraging me to seek success and to strive for more and to believe for more. That's not the background I came from. So having to deal with that reality—especially in light of the world's assumptions about our "perfect" family—has been incredibly isolating. So instead of saying, "Yeah, my family life isn't great," I have often remained silent and swallowed the pain.

When my parents came to the orphanage that I grew up in, they weren't even there to adopt any children. They were in China to pick up my adopted sister, who was five hours away from where I was. A family who lived down the street from them had also adopted a Chinese baby, but from my orphanage in Nanjing. So the family asked my parents if they would drive to the Nanjing orphanage to check in on her.

My parents thought, *While we're here, we'll just tour the whole orphanage.* And during that tour, they came to the five-to-ten-year-olds' room where I was living along with about fifty other kids. We were all sitting around a table, so my parents couldn't see that I was missing a leg. They came over and tried to speak to me, which was more like waving and giving each other a thumbs-up, and they felt a connection with me. So they inquired about me and another little boy they had seen in my orphanage.

They started the adoption process almost by accident. About six months later, they received a call from the adoption agency and the agent said, "You know that little girl you want? Well, she's missing her right 'shank.'" That's the term they used—not at all discriminatory, right? Just call it a leg!

My parents had no idea I was missing any limb, so they went through all the videos and all the photos, trying to figure out what a "shank" was. Finally, they realized what the agent meant—I had no right leg. So they talked it over and instead of my disability deterring them, they were even more determined to get me. They wanted to help me. And for that, I will be eternally grateful. It takes an incredible set of people to be willing to bring a grown kid with a disability into their home. This was way before prosthetics were advanced or even widely available. So to help out a child with a physical disability when your resources are limited is an incredibly generous act. I commend my parents so much for being willing to take me on.

It seemed they struggled to raise me. I don't think they realized how much my disability would affect their own lives. And that's really no fault of their own; it's just the world we lived in, and to some degree, still live in today. People with disabilities have never been very visible.

We went through significant growing pains together. Whereas my sister and my brother, who were adopted at sixteen months and five years old, didn't struggle as much. I always felt like the family drain—the family wet blanket.

"We can't do that because Scout can't..." fill in the blank.

As I got older, I'm sure I drove my parents crazy by constantly talking about my dreams and goals. I think on one hand, they just aren't wired to think that way. They loved life in a small town, enjoyed their routines, and didn't seem to long for more. On the other hand, when I would say, "I can't wait to get out of this town and make something of myself," it was probably offensive. So they were both put off and confused. "Why can't you just be content where you are?" my dad would say. I didn't have those answers.

I grew up feeling like I was on one team and my parents and siblings were on another. There was loneliness, yes. There were feelings of rejection and the ever-present reminder that I wasn't like anyone else in my home or community. Since then, not much has changed. I know that's probably disappointing, but that's just life. Not every happy ending means we get what we want. Some happy endings aren't happy at all. They come in the form of radical acceptance and a complete release of expectations.

What *has* improved are my boundaries.

Sometimes, when relationships are consistently disappointing and difficult, it's okay to create healthy space and distance that allows you to be who you are and allows them to be who they are without causing turmoil or drama. I don't answer my phone every time it rings and neither do they. I have girlfriends who call their moms or sisters every day, multiple times a day. That's not my reality and that's okay. I've been incredibly lucky to have women and girls placed in my life who make that loneliness a little less pressing.

IDENTITY CRISIS

We've already talked about my years in elementary and middle school, where growing up in a white, conservative community left me feeling like I was on some sort of social treadmill that made it impossible to gain any ground. And by the time I got to high school, I was *done* with my hometown. I think a lot of people come to that place—where they're ready for whatever's next.

I remember being in high school thinking, *If I can just get to what's next. If I can just get to college. Get out of this town. Get around different people—people like me. Then I won't feel lonely anymore. I won't feel left out. I'll find my place of belonging.*

I was wrong.

My first year of college felt like a yearlong tightrope walk. Coming out of a small town where everyone thought and valued the same things, I thought I was ready to take on the world. I thought I was ready to discover new ideas, meet people from around the world, and have that transformative "college experience" you hear about people having.

I underestimated how personally challenging it would be to reshape my perspectives, faith, and beliefs.

I spent most of the first year terrified. In fact, there were times I thought to myself, *I'm not going to make it here. I should just go home.* I hadn't realized *just* how sheltered I'd been until my first biology class where the professor announced that Creationism had no place in science, and that if we wanted to be taken seriously, we would leave our "parents' faith" at the door to his classroom and begin using our logic instead. Like, this was in his lecture on day one.

I also had a difficult time making friends. I guess I'd watched too many early 2000s movies about college, but I had this assumption that we'd all just sort of like, meet up in the "quad" and hang out discussing art and philosophy before heading out to the biggest Greek party on campus. That is not, shockingly, how it works. For the most part, I was homesick. Not in the sense that I missed my parents or my siblings, and not even in the sense that I realized something great about my hometown. It was more that I missed what was familiar.

That year at UCLA was the beginning of my understanding of how big and complex our world is. I know that sounds stupid, because obviously I cognitively understood that people believed differently than I did, but I underestimated the vast differences I had never experienced. People with different political beliefs, different sexual orientations, different opinions, different values, different faiths. I also became aware of the sufferings and injustices that are present around the world. Nanjing, China, was kind to me compared to what many others have endured.

It was a year of identity crisis. In many ways, I felt very uncomfortable, just trying to wrestle with the idea that everything I had been taught might not be the truth—or at least, the truth as I was beginning to perceive it. It was also the year that I realized how "whitewashed" my racial identity was. Up until then, I would have identified more as a white person than an

Asian. Around 40 percent of UCLA students are Asian, and I saw how proud they were to be Asian. How they kept many of the Asian traditions and customs, and how most of them were still fluent in Chinese or Mandarin or whatever language was spoken in their country.

I was embarrassed at how very little I knew about my own heritage and culture.

On the other hand, I wanted to respect the white family and community that raised me. Without my parents, I wouldn't be in the United States, so I didn't want to completely discount the values and traditions they'd passed on to me. I felt caught between two worlds, which is a very lonely place to be, because if you're not "in" with one group, it feels like you're in neither. I wondered, *Is it possible to have this duality of being both? Do I have to be white or Asian? Can I embrace both worlds at the same time without selling out?*

I don't think I'm alone in this experience, either. Many of us grow up in homes with certain values, beliefs, and traditions, and we come to a point later in life where we begin to question the things we've always generally accepted as fact. I can't tell you how many girls I've mentored who have come to me and said, "Scout, I don't know what I believe anymore." And I understand how hard that can be—how isolating it can feel to have your foundation shift beneath you like that. We so deeply connect what we think to who we are, because if my core beliefs aren't true, what does that say about me?

To any of you going through an identity crisis or a crisis of faith, I'd say this: Keep thinking for yourself. Ultimately, you're the one who has to live with your values—you're the one who is charged with living those out. It's okay to take beliefs and ideas from different groups and different sides of debates, and then hang on to the ones that ring true for you.

LONELY AS A LESSON

I was kind of a late bloomer. I didn't have a boyfriend in high school or anything, but like a lot of people, I got my first serious boyfriend in college. Again, I thought, *This is it. I won't feel lonely now. I've got someone. I'm in a relationship.* And, again, I was wrong. I've been lonely single and lonely in love, and I'd argue that relationship loneliness is far, far worse.

I think many of us have this expectation that being with someone is going to fix something for us—most of all, loneliness. And I'm not going to lie—it feels nice to wake up to that "Good morning" text and to have someone to eat dinner with on a random Tuesday night when you don't want to be alone. But ultimately, being in a relationship is not the cure for loneliness, either.

If I could give you one lesson I've learned about loneliness, it would be this: If you'll let it, loneliness can be one of those most useful and positively catalytic experiences of your life.

See, when we experience loneliness, we have a flight-or-fight response. Which makes sense. It doesn't feel good to be lonely.

We feel uncomfortable. It's human nature to want to relieve discomfort. In some cases, loneliness can feel both helpless and hopeless—the way I felt after Hope left. But if you choose to embrace it, loneliness can be a phenomenal life coach. Because for me, it allowed me to figure out where I needed to be better, where I needed to grow, and what I could do to change my perspective and my circumstances.

Maybe I felt really lonely that first year in college because I didn't really find the right group to connect to. I didn't really find *my* people. But my loneliness forced me to ask, *What am I doing to change my circumstances? What can I do better? How can I grow right now? Am I making the effort to connect? To open up? To invite?*

I think a lot of my loneliness growing up was because I'm actually quite timid and reserved by nature. People reading this who know me now will probably laugh, but it's true. I was born an introvert. Being a social person is a learned behavior—a skill I developed because I realized that no one can do anything about my loneliness but me. Of course it's scary to put yourself out there—it's still scary for me sometimes! But unless you make an effort to create relationships, it's not very likely they'll organically spring up around you.

I know this is like the least breaking news ever, but I love sports. *Love*, love them. All of them. If you were to walk into my apartment at any given time, you'd hear a game or ESPN playing on the TV in the background. So, early in my sophomore year, I was in my dorm and I walked past an open door of a room full of guys. I overheard one of them talking about the football game.

I kept walking, but then just down the hallway I paused. *You should go say something,* I told myself. *You should ask if they're watching the game tonight.* I was terrified to be that vulnerable, especially to a room full of dudes, but I was more terrified to stay lonely. Slowly, I walked back to the door and knocked.

"Hey guys..." My heart was racing, so I hesitated to finish the thought—worried my voice would do something stupid like quiver. I had their attention—six pairs of eyes stared back at me.

Speak Scout, speak. "Would it be okay if I came in?" I asked.

They were looking at me like, *Wait. You're a chick—and you want to come into this room full of guys?* I could tell they were confused.

"I heard you guys talking about the football game," I said. "Are you watching it together? Would it be cool if I came by to watch, too?"

I prayed the floor would open beneath me and swallow me up, I was so scared. But these guys were totally down. "Yeah, sure."

I could tell they were surprised, but I could also tell they were curious about this girl who invited herself to watch a football game. And we had a great time! I won't say that the experience led me to lifelong friendships with any of those guys, but it was one less lonely night and a lesson in taking a risk to confront my own loneliness.

That was one of the first bold moves I had to make to overcome loneliness. In fact, I think that most of the brave and courageous things I've done in my life, most of the experiences from which I grew, the biggest transformations I've undergone, have come from a season or seasons of loneliness. A lot of the things that I'm most grateful for and appreciate the most today have come from places of loneliness—like training. Training isn't a team sport. And even though I'm around other people while I train doesn't mean I'm engaging in interactions with them beyond a surface level. But obviously, that type of loneliness is worth it to me because it allows me to do what I love—compete.

If you can reframe what loneliness means, it can become a season that allows you to reflect, to reevaluate, and to assess. And then you can choose to adjust and prioritize your life based on what you need most. Sometimes, that might be to remain isolated so you can grind out a skill, learning, or development. And sometimes, that might mean walking past a room full of dudes and inviting yourself to their watch party.

LONELY VERSUS ALONE

For young women, so much of loneliness is attached to singleness, right? And the idea that, if you're single, you're lonely. While that's understandable, and I have felt that at times, I have also—in hindsight—really appreciated my singleness. I'm not a serial dater. I haven't been in a lot of relationships because the most important thing about me is not my relationship status. The most important thing about me is what I'm doing with my life and how I'm using my voice to help others. The same is true for you—you're far more significant than a title. You don't have to be lonely if you're working toward your dreams. If you have your eyes set on things above and things ahead, if you're ambitious and you're driven and living a life of purpose, if you're rooted in who you are, you rarely ever feel lonely.

Look—it's taken me a while to get here. Where I can be okay being single and with not having a traditional partner. It's taken a lot of work, but I've had a perspective change. Right? *How can I grow? How can I improve? What matters most right now?* I can use this time to build for the future, to work on myself, to see the world, to create new passions, and to work on my craft.

When you are able to become more focused on who you're becoming instead of who you're dating, you don't feel alone. You feel empowered.

One of the main differences I've learned as I've gotten older is that being lonely is different from being alone. While I have felt lonely at times, I know that in my heart I've never been alone because I've always had God on this journey with me. That's my belief—my faith. And I'm convinced of it. But if God isn't your thing, I'd suggest you spend some time sorting out your spiritual beliefs based on your own convictions. We all need a deeper connection with something bigger than we are to ground us. And without my faith, those seasons of loneliness would have felt a lot more like despair.

THE WRONG MEDICINE

One of the quickest ways to limit your future is to allow your loneliness to steer the direction of your life. I've seen some of my friends make the dumbest choices out of loneliness. I've seen girls give up their physical boundaries out of loneliness and then suffer for it. I've seen people in toxic relationships who stay in an unhealthy cycle to avoid it. I've seen people get married and divorced quickly. I've even seen athletes give up their careers because of it.

I've seen countless people trade in their potential to avoid what it feels like to sit with themselves in isolation.

Whatever you're using to fill the space of loneliness in your life, it will take on greater meaning than it would otherwise. For me, training, mentoring, and advocacy have been my answer to loneliness—which now doesn't feel like loneliness at all. But there was a time when I would sit on social media and scroll through the lives of others, comparing myself and feeding my loneliness until it grew, and grew, and grew. Then, I was painfully aware that I was lonely.

Do you see the difference? When you're just so focused on doing you, and you're not trying to find somebody, you're not trying to attach your loneliness to a relationship, status, or title, good things happen. Good things come into your life. And "lonely" isn't a word in your vocabulary.

THE LONELY THAT HURTS

I think in its own way, loneliness always hurts. It stings. It makes us squirm. It's a feeling we want to go away, but still a feeling we can live with. But there are other levels of lonely that can be especially painful and lead us to extreme mindsets that, left on their own over time, can be dangerous.

The global pandemic ushered in some of the most critical cases of loneliness our country (and the entire world) has ever experienced. In a recently published survey of American adults, almost 40 percent reported having feelings of "serious loneliness."[1] But the number that really troubles me is 63—the percentage of young adults who are experiencing significant symptoms of anxiety or depression.

I get messages all the time from people who are hurting—who are in acute pain simply because they are lonely. I wish I could respond to every one of them. In fact, I wish I could hug the person behind the message. I know it's a scary time to feel untethered. I've struggled with my own mental health at different periods in my life, and I can promise you this—I have never regretted opening up to someone and telling them what's going on. Never.

Why? Because it's important to identify whether your loneliness is the manageable, short-term variety, or if it could potentially be something more dangerous, often called chronic loneliness. Since I'm *not* a medical professional, I've researched a list of signs of chronic loneliness from a number of reputable resources.

But before I even get to that, I want to tell you that if you're unsure whether or not your loneliness is chronic, I beg you to *get help*. Reach out to someone right now. Put this book down and make a call, send a text, get an appointment, set up a meeting. Your life has value and if you feel otherwise, there's absolutely no shame in consulting a professional. In fact, I've learned that the words "I need help" are some of the most powerful words in any language.

If you don't have the resources to speak to a professional, tell someone. Anyone. Get in an online support group. Don't suffer in silence.

I asked licensed professional counselor and national certified counselor Dr. Chinwe Williams what the differences were between an average person's loneliness and someone whose loneliness might be described as chronic. You might be experiencing chronic loneliness if you have consistent feelings of *some or all* of the following:

Your interactions with others aren't fulfilling. You struggle to connect with others on a deep, intimate level. Engagement with family and friends feels forced or at a very surface level. Therefore you crave authentic connections.

You don't ever feel seen. You may have one or two close friends but don't feel like they truly understand or "get" you. You spend all day with people but still feel isolated and alone. You can walk around outside on a busy street, or be surrounded by tons of people on a busy train or at a concert but feel invisible or as if you are in a bubble. Feeling "alone" almost feels like your default setting.

Desire to binge-watch shows. Research from the University of Texas found that chronic loneliness can lead to an increased desire to binge-watch television shows or movies. While many people do this, participants reported this as a distraction from feelings of loneliness and isolation.

Negative feelings of self-doubt and self-worth. Constantly feeling inadequate or less than enough. For some, chasing or clinging emotionally to others. Over time, these feelings are possible symptoms of chronic loneliness.

Lack of hope. Long-term loneliness can lead to sadness, depression, and eventually despair—an inability to find any hope that things will get better.

Chronic loneliness has been linked to an increased risk of heart disease, stroke, and suicide.[2] If you saw your life reflected in the list above, don't wait. Get help. I'm already proud of your using your voice to fight for your life.

THE CURE FOR LONELY

As we've learned together (me, the hard way), there is no simple cure for loneliness. But there are strategies and coping tools we can use to manage the self-defeating thoughts and behaviors that fuel those feelings of isolation and hopelessness.

From my own experience, here's how to keep loneliness from limiting your future:

1. Admit when you're lonely. Being lonely is an unavoidable part of the human experience. Admit it to yourself. And, if needed, admit it to someone else.

2. Ask yourself, *What can I learn from this experience? How can I get better? What can I do to overcome these feelings of loneliness?*

3. Stay focused on *you*. When you're pursuing your own dreams and ambitions, loneliness doesn't really exist because you realize that who you're becoming is more important than who you're dating.

4. Don't be afraid to put yourself out there when the time is right. Whose football party do you need to crash? Take a risk and make meaningful connections that you can lean into when life gets challenging.

5. Remember, you're not alone. Invest in your spiritual self. If you're not sure what you believe, do your

research. Spend time in meditation. Read. Talk to God. In my experience, He's always been the best medicine for my loneliness.

I've never experienced loneliness like I did when I lost Hope. But today I have a different kind of hope—a hope in myself. A hope that I have a purpose to serve and an irreplaceable role to play. I believe the same is true for you. The cure to your loneliness is just one hope away.

CHAPTER FIVE

BODY IMAGE

I distinctly remember being a little girl in line at the grocery store and seeing a *Self* magazine cover with Cindy Crawford on it. The ad copy on the front said something about getting "the legs you'll love." I couldn't have felt more alienated. For one, Cindy Crawford was (and still is) a beauty icon. More than that, Cindy Crawford was the absolute standard. She was the measuring stick. Tall, thin, white...with two legs—legs "you'll love."

I left the grocery store feeling sick to my stomach. *Why do I have to look this way?* I wondered. *Why can't I be beautiful? Will anybody ever be able to love me?*

After that day, I would go on to spend the next two decades at war with my body.

SHORT STUFF

Can we be real with each other? We've spent four chapters together already, and I think it's time that I just lay out some truths for you about the body of Scout Bassett.

I'm four feet nine inches tall—or short, I guess I should say.

I have scars from burns from my waist down. Like, when I wear a swimsuit, from the backside, all you see are burn remnants on my bum and my thighs, stretching down to my hamstrings and legs. I remember being in a swimsuit for the first time and catching sight of myself in the mirror and thinking, *That rear view really is so unpleasant.*

On the foot I do have, I have four toes—my big toe is gone. There's scar tissue compacted at the bottom of that foot, too, which was also badly burned in the fire I was involved in as an infant. I mean, feet are ugly to look at anyway, but when you've got all these additional differences, it really does you zero favors.

It was sort of funny last year when I went to the orthopedic surgeon. I was having trouble with my foot, and when I took off my sock to show him, he visibly flinched. *Wasn't expecting that, huh?* I wanted to say. Instead, my insanely clever response was, "Yeah. There are only four toes."

And this *astounding* wit is probably why Scout's still single.

I've been on photo shoots before where the makeup artist has tried to even out the skin tone where I'm burned. It's taken me a long, long time, but I now ask them to leave the burns alone. I was on the set of a shoot for a magazine that was publishing an interview with me on body image and the makeup artist started airbrushing my legs. I actually jumped out of the spray, shocked.

"This is silly," I told her. "I can't tell girls to be comfortable with their bodies while I'm airbrushed into a blur." Like, come on. That's completely disingenuous. In this makeup artist's defense, she felt so bad. She apologized right away. She's just so used to breaking out the airbrush that it was a rote response for her. She was probably thinking, *Oh, this will make Scout feel better.* I fully believe her intentions were good. But this is the world and the culture that we live in—where covering any imperfection is a knee-jerk reaction.

If I'm honest, I'm less self-conscious about my missing leg and more self-conscious about my burns and my height—or lack of height. Because if it's not the leg jokes, it's the short people jokes. And there is no shortage of short people jokes. Trust me. I've heard them all—twice.

It was brutal growing up. Every day I went to school, somebody would make some sort of joke about me being short. I'd always get (and sometimes still get), "Oh, are you a 'little person'?" If I were, that would be totally fine. But the question can be offensive because their intention, often evident in the tone of the question, is to judge me, hurt me, and belittle me.

I think my height has been especially hard to deal with because of my line of work. It's not an advantage in sprinting to be four foot nine. I'm running against girls who are a torso, head, and shoulders taller than I am. If you look at the photo from the 2022 Nationals, you can tell the photographers had a difficult time getting me and the runners on either side of me in the pictures. It's laughable. In the past, it was a daily struggle to not torture myself by thinking, *Oh, if I was just a little bit taller, I'd be even better. I'd be even faster.*

So much of the beauty and fashion industry is built around this false sense of perfection. When we see these images, we're made to feel less than. *I'll never look like that,* we'll think. When the truth is those models and celebrities don't even look like that. But there is no other sector that I'm aware of where more of a prejudice exists against people who have bodily imperfections or deformities. You don't see a lot of people in wheelchairs on magazine covers. You definitely don't see a lot of amputees.

THE PRESSURE OF PERFECTION

Moving into my late twenties, my body image was at rock bottom. I went down a total spiral of depression, anxiety, and panic attacks. It was rough. At first, I avoided seeking help because I felt like I had already overcome so much in my life. I considered myself to be a strong person. Surely, I could just get over my insecurity and anxiety on my own, right? But I was struggling with deep pain and depression, in some ways, a kind of grief I couldn't shake. There was still all this unprocessed trauma.

I started to gain weight. Then 2020 happened and all the gyms in my area shut down. Despite finding random public parks to train in, my weight continued to rise. I wasn't at my healthiest by a long shot. When I came back to racing in 2021, I got beat. There's a guy who is a teammate of mine who was sitting in the stands within earshot of my friend who was recording my race on her phone. When I saw the video, I could hear him in the background saying all kinds of crazy stuff.

"Oh my God, look at Scout getting beat. She's so fat now. She's out of shape. No wonder she's losing. She's deadweight!"

My friend told me later that she had stopped recording to have a little "chat" with this dude. "You need to shut your mouth," she told him. "You have no idea what her story is or what she's gone through recently."

What's ironic about all of this is that now he's very vocal about mental health after being diagnosed with bipolar disorder. I guess my friend is right—we rarely know the entirety of someone's story.

After a trip back to China in 2016, I was in a dark place. My doctor recommended I start taking antidepressants. I didn't want to do it. It felt like losing, somehow. But I knew I couldn't manage the feelings of misery and despair, so I gave the medicine a shot. One side effect of some antidepressants is gaining weight. So it felt like I was battling a hundred different things now. I was struggling to find the right medication for me, and my body felt alien.

I remember one afternoon I had gotten back from training and had soaked in the bath. I got out and stared at myself in the floor-length mirror. I looked at my body and began to pick myself apart. From my weird foot, to the missing leg, to the burns, to the pudgy stomach and swollen face. I weighed more than I'd ever weighed in my entire life. I looked at the girl staring back at me and I said, "You're disgusting."

And I meant it. I was revolted by my body.

There were photos taken of me during that time—magazine covers, article features, ads. I remember a spot I did for Abercrombie & Fitch in particular when I knew I didn't look or feel my best. After the ad came out I walked into the training center one afternoon to find a group of girls in the locker room huddled over a phone, presumably looking at one of these pictures. "She doesn't look good at *all*," one said. I knew they were talking about me. I didn't call them out or stand up for myself because, you know what? I agreed with them.

For my more "mature" readers, maybe you can relate to this experience—as a woman, I had no idea how much my body would change after I turned thirty. Before I hit thirty, I ate whatever I wanted and I never gained a pound. I could eat a burrito and go to practice—no problem. I'd always been thin. Even when I didn't work out, I'd always had definition, presumably from genetics. I'd never had a weight problem growing up all the way through my twenties. Almost the *day* I turned thirty, everything changed. My hormones changed. My body composition changed. My metabolism changed. As an athlete, I had to navigate the new concept that I couldn't eat the same way. I couldn't do the same things. This change on top of the dark place I was in mentally and emotionally felt like a huge weight. It felt like lying beneath a boulder, waiting for my lungs to give out.

It's a cruel reality to live in, but people justify their judgment because I'm an athlete. My body is my tool. I'm a *sprinter*. I'm "supposed" to be thin. I'm "supposed" to be fit. I know celebrities who *aren't* athletes experience this, too—the pressure of perfection. But I don't think I realized just how pervasive this pressure is until I began my work with my mentees with the Challenged Athletes Foundation. These kids—some as young as under ten years old—are struggling with that same pressure of perfection.

It made me wonder...where does that even come from?

So I put on my nerd cap, and I did a little research. Here's what I found: Our obsession with perfection is both dangerous and on the rise.

I don't know how many times I've heard this: "Oh, I'm such a perfectionist. Like, it's *so* annoying." Really? Is it just *so tough* being *so perfect*? I'm the worst, but that phrase annoys me: "I'm just *such* a perfectionist."

And maybe you are. But that's not something to brag about. In fact, it's becoming an increasingly alarming confession.

We tend to hold up perfectionism as some sort of life trophy—the more perfect we appear, the higher quality of human we are. But, as psychologist Thomas Curran points out, perfectionists are no more successful than anyone else.[1] In fact, the opposite is true. If you're a perfectionist, you probably struggle to ever feel content or satisfied. You probably find it difficult to be at ease, and you're probably chasing impossible outcomes that leave you feeling like you're always *just shy* of all your goals.

But that's not where the dangers of perfectionism end. In fact, those are the mild symptoms of our country's pressure-of-perfection epidemic. In a study published in 2019 by the American Psychological Association, we learn that "Research among college students and young people...has found...perfectionism to be positively associated with clinical depression, anorexia nervosa, and early death...It is also associated with greater physiological reactivity (e.g., elevated blood pressure) and illbeing (e.g., negative affect) in response to life stress and failure...The ill-effects of...perfectionism are substantiated in recent comprehensive reviews, which found that this dimension of perfectionism positively correlates with suicide ideation and predicts increases in depression over time..."[2]

I'm sorry, what? When I started reading about all the residual side effects of perfectionism, it made me want to eradicate the word from my vocabulary. Depression, eating disorders, high blood pressure, suicidal thoughts, and *premature death*? Those aren't your mama's side effects, friends. Those are serious. As serious as they can possibly be. And while I'm not trying to usher in doom-and-gloom thinking, the obsession with perfection is only getting worse, rising steadily in the United States, Canada, and the United Kingdom for the better part of the last three decades.[3]

So, what are we supposed to do about it? How can we push back against this ideal that, in order to be happy, successful, or valuable, we must also be perfect? Well, that's one of the reasons I wanted to write this book. I didn't want to just tell my story. I wanted to incite change while giving girls and women practical advice on navigating the challenges we all face as females on planet Earth. And this, the last "adversity" we'll discuss together, is one of the hottest topics in my inbox.

"How are you so confident?" one girl messaged me.

"I'm an Asian in an all-white school," another wrote. "How did you survive?"

"I want to work out, but I don't have the time or energy," read another DM. "I hate my body."

SILENCE THE INNER CRITIC

It took me four years to reclaim my body as something useful, beautiful, and good. I have finally gotten to a much healthier and better place. But I've done a lot of work. That's not to say that I don't still have my moments of insecurity. Whether it's gaining a little weight, or whether it's the burns, my height, my foot, my missing leg—I'm just as aware of those truths about me as I ever was. I'm not asking you to pretend things aren't true about you or your body. That's silly and unrealistic.

But what I am asking you to do is to be in control of your own thoughts and the way you talk to yourself. First of all, one realization I had to come to is it's okay to figure yourself out. I was going through a lot—a *lot* when I packed on the pounds. But that was my right to do so. I didn't have to drop the weight based on anyone else's timeline. And I'm glad that I didn't. I met my body where it was at and I dealt with what mattered most—my mental game. Ultimately, *that's* where we all need to start. Our own minds.

I had a reconstruction surgeon reach out to me not long ago and say, "I do a lot of work with burn victims and would be happy to consult with you on revising some of your burn scars. If you're ever interested in cosmetic surgery, let me know. I'll give you a deal."

My first reaction was, *Are you crazy, dude? I'm not going under the knife!* I've had enough nonelective surgery to know that any surgery is major surgery. Recovery times are rarely what you think they'll be, and the fewer times that I have to go under anesthesia, the better. You never know what can happen, even in a cosmetic procedure.

But I think the more pervasive thought I had was, *No, I earned these scars.* I know that may sound weird to you, but after all I'd been through, these burns are now as much a part of me as my running blade, as my face, as my hands. They're *mine.* They serve as a beautiful and powerful reminder of everything I've experienced and everything I've overcome.

When you can look down at yourself and see what you've survived and what you've been able to do with your life despite your imperfections, those imperfections become an important character in that narrative. They become something you're able to embrace instead of something you want to change. Now, these burns are symbolic. They don't make me feel ugly anymore. They make me feel powerful. They make me feel like a warrior.

I got to this place slowly. Like I said, it took four long years of wrestling with my identity and my body to get here. Yes, the anti-depressants helped for a time. The therapy helped for a time. But what has sustained me for the long haul is that I've learned to silence the inner critic—the nagging echo of my voice constantly telling me I'm not good enough, pretty enough, or thin enough. I'm inviting you to do the same. This takes practice, but I'm telling you, it's been the key to the doors of confidence and body acceptance.

I bet if you were to write down every thought you have about yourself—and especially the thoughts you have about the way you look—you'd be shocked. You'd realize that the biggest bully in your life is probably you. The way we talk to ourselves is actually atrocious. It's abusive and it's sad. One of the biggest lessons I've learned about body image is that I'm the only person who can change the way I view myself.

I can date a guy who thinks I'm gorgeous and tells me all the time. That may improve my body image temporarily, but those thoughts and insecurities will come back. I lost the weight I gained during the COVID-19 lockdown, but then I found new things to dislike about myself. We can "patch up" our body image, but what we really need is a body image overhaul.

That starts with controlling your thoughts. The best method I've found to do this is to immediately counter any negative critique of my body with something positive that's true. For example, if I say, "I hate the way I look in a bathing suit," I'll immediately counter with, "But I've got great arms. And I look strong and powerful."

Or if I say, "These pants fit tighter than they used to. I'm getting fat again," I'll counter it with, "It could be that I'm gaining muscle. I have been lifting heavier at the gym."

"I hate my nose." Countered with, "My face is defined and unique. No one in the world has a face like mine."

Look, some of this sounds awkward. I get it. This isn't an after-school special "feel good" book. Some of this work is hard and some of this work feels uncomfortable. All I'm asking is that you *try*. That you commit to thirty days of replacing negative thoughts with positive thoughts. Even if the only positive thing you can say about your body is, "It's keeping me alive today." It's a start.

Silence the inner critic. Don't let your body image limit your joy, limit your influence, or limit your life.

SILENCING THE OUTER CRITIC

There isn't a whole lot I can add to the conversation on bullying that hasn't already been said except to talk about my own experience.

I've already detailed how other kids would tease and mock me. The jokes, the sneers, even the inappropriate questions: "Can

I touch your fake leg?" Like, you wouldn't ask an able-bodied person if you can caress their knee, would you? No. I'd like to say that moments like these have been isolated to my childhood, but that's not the case. I still face plenty of public scrutiny both as a female and as a professional athlete (as evidenced by my own teammate ripping me apart on camera).

When I was younger, though, the body critics made me feel so isolated. Like I was the only one being singled out and bullied. But as an educated adult, I know almost one in four kids from ages twelve to eighteen are bullied.[4] And that's just *reported* bullying. I'm sure that number is actually much higher. In fact, I bet all of us at some point have been made to feel outwardly less than by someone or some social construct.

My advice to silencing the outer critics is to channel their negativity into fuel. To leverage their words to make you *better* not *bitter*. I can't say that I haven't thought about some of those kids, teachers, and coaches who underestimated me when I line up on the track. It feels good to prove them wrong. That's not my motivation in competing, but it would be a lie to say that their words and behaviors toward me haven't pushed me a little harder and a little faster.

Maybe for you it is time to move your body. It is time to switch out fast food for something healthier. Instead of letting their words bring you down, let their words push you and fuel you. Prove them wrong. Adopt better habits. Not for them, but for *you* to feel your best.

Or maybe you dress a little differently and people like to point this out in a way that makes you feel self-conscious. You're an artist. You like fashion. And you like to push the boundaries of both. Get online and find classes in beauty and fashion. Take a makeup class. Go to cosmetology school.

The greatest lesson I've learned from my outside critics is that the things that make me "different" are also the things that set me apart. They make me distinct. Noticeable. They're the things that make me stand out in a crowd. In a world where so many people are trying to be the same thing, being different is your superpower.

Invest in your differences. Those are the things that give you the potential to be great.

BODY ISSUES

In 2019 I was invited to be featured in *ESPN*'s Body Issue. My first response? Oh, hell no. There was no way. I had no desire to expose my body and its burns and scars. I'd seen Body Issue photographs of other athletes before. The idea terrified me. But I had this nagging feeling tugging me back toward the invitation. The idea of helping to promote greater visibility for people with disabilities changed my mind. Sometimes, we have to put aside our own fears and be willing to take the lead and to be bold and courageous. Not just for ourselves, but for somebody else.

Saying yes was a big deal for me for a number of reasons. For one, to be featured in any issue of *ESPN* magazine is major. To have the honor of representing both Asian Americans and people with disabilities is something I don't take lightly. And two...I posed nude. Naked. Fully in the buff. Not a stitch of apparel in sight.

For the first time, my burns and my missing leg and my weird foot were exposed for all the world to see. And it felt *exhilarating*. Truly. It really did! I couldn't believe how empowered and confident I felt. Not just because I was naked in front of millions of readers, but because I was able to share my story and my passion for advocacy and change for disabled athletes—especially female disabled athletes.

Because they need to see someone who looks like them in a magazine. Girls with missing limbs come up to me all the time and say, "Oh, I don't know if I want to do running, because the blades are kind of ugly." I understand their perspective—that's how I viewed the running blade the first time I was fitted for one. But I'm also heartbroken by their reluctance to give it a shot. Because for me, that was the moment I became Scout Bassett.

So I'll tell them, "Just try it. It's not how it looks that matters. It's how it makes you *feel*."

I want girls to see the running blade and think, *Wow. That's an emblem of power. Of beauty. Of might.* I want them to see the places you can go and the things you can overcome through sport. I want girls with missing limbs to see a running blade and think, *Man, I gotta have one of those. Running blades are badass. And they're my ticket to a limitless future.*

FULL CIRCLE

Remember the Cindy Crawford cover on *Self* magazine that jumpstarted my insecurities? Well, in 2021, *I* was on the cover of *Self* magazine. It was my first cover.

I know. It's crazy—totally full circle.

The cover didn't matter to me because of the attention or the recognition I received. It mattered to me because it continues to give girls a new standard—or maybe because it's beginning to tear down all standards. That would be my ultimate goal.

Later that same year, something else incredible happened. American Girl Doll created a Team USA line that included a doll inspired by yours truly, complete with a running blade. I couldn't freaking believe it. If I could go back and tell that little girl in the grocery line that one day she'd have her own doll, there's no way she'd believe me. And you know what? I'm glad I can't. Because the journey ahead of her had meaning and purpose. The transformation she would endure was both brutal and beautiful.

But what I can do is tell *you* right now that there is so much more to you than flesh and bone and hair. *So much more.* But more importantly, there is great value in your flesh and bone and hair. Your body is your instrument. The Bible says that your body is the temple God's Spirit lives in. It also says that you were bought with a price—because of Christ's sacrifice (1 Corinthians 6:19–20 NIV). I believe that. Your body is a gift. It carries you. It animates you. It sustains you. It houses your soul.

So, what if you don't look like Cindy Crawford. Or Gigi Hadid. Or a Kardashian? The truth is, those girls don't really look like that, either. They have teams—teams for their teams—that help them achieve their look. Don't get me wrong, they're beautiful girls. But I know for a fact they have insecurities of their own that they have to work through, too.

Between seeing the Cindy Crawford cover and seeing my own *Self* cover, there was so much growth. Some of it excruciating, but all worth it.

CHAPTER SIX

YOUR WHY

When I was growing up, I didn't know exactly what I wanted to do for a career. A lot of times you'll ask a kid what they want to be when they grow up and they'll say a doctor, a teacher, an astronaut. They know. Whether they actually accomplish those goals is one thing, but they have a specific idea of what job sounds appealing to them. I wasn't like that—I just knew I wanted something different from what most of the people in my town had. I wanted to do something big with my life—something great.

But if I had to have answered this question as a kid, I would have said that I wanted to do something in politics. That's right—Scout Bassett for president! I told you I was sort of a nerd already, but now you're really about to see just how deep in the dork waters I swam.

One of my favorite pastimes as a kid was reading. I was absolutely voracious. I would devour books in a single sitting and then ask my mom to take me to the library to get more. One of my favorite types of books to read was political biographies. I read about John Adams, Henry Kissinger, Colin Powell, Bill Clinton. But one of my favorite books of all time has been *The Art of Negotiation: How to Improvise Agreement in a Chaotic World* by Michael Wheeler. That book made me want to work for the State Department.

Looking back, I'm sure it was pure comedy watching me walk down the hallway in fourth and fifth grade holding a poli-sci book that was eight hundred pages thick. Honestly, some of these books were half my body weight. I'm also sure my affinity for reading did *not* increase my status in the social hierarchy. Not by a long shot. I'm sure people were like, *Okay. This Asian girl with a disability reading about the history of American politics? This chick is crazy.*

But I brought books with me everywhere. When I was twelve years old, my parents took me to see Stan Patterson, a prosthetic specialist who is certified by the American Board for Certification in Orthotics, Prosthetics and Pedorthics. In other words, he's the most badass limb-maker since God himself.

I was there because I was a very active kid, in addition to all the reading I did, and my activeness was especially challenging because I was limited by my everyday prosthetic. So my parents took me to Stan in hopes of finding me a prosthetic that would allow me to do more and compete in sports better than with my everyday prosthetic—one I could run on, pivot on, and make quicker movements on.

When I met Stan, I was reading Barbara Bush's biography. I remember him noticing the book and being like, *What in the world is going on here?* I laugh about it every time I think about his baffled expression.

I was *super* into global affairs, too. I watched the news. I had subscriptions to newspapers and online media outlets. I was fascinated by the way the world's governments worked—or didn't work. For the longest time—and this shows you just how naive I was—I thought I wanted a career in politics. And if you would have asked the people who knew me at the time, I'm sure they would have said, "Oh, Scout's going to be a politician. Or an ambassador. She's going to do some kind of work at the State Department."

Spoiler alert: I didn't go into politics. By the time I got to college, my views had started to shift. Like I've already told you, I grew up with very conservative values, beliefs, and even politics. But when I got to UCLA, it was like a filter had been removed from my vision. Instead of viewing the world as black and white, I began to see everything in color.

POLITICS OF FAITH

Since then, I've wrestled with finding my *own* truth. With determining how my faith influences how I view and treat other people. I'll give you an example. Growing up, I was always taught that homosexuality is a sin. That it's unbiblical. Had I gone into politics without attending UCLA, I would have been staunchly anti-same-sex marriage. But when I went to college, I started to meet people who were LGBTQ. They are wonderful people—some of the best. So my perspective and my heart began to change.

I've also had a chance to travel the world since my early love affair with politics. I've been able to witness the incredible amount of suffering and discrimination people have endured in the name of God and religion.

On the other side of that spectrum is another experience I had at UCLA. There's a tradition there called the Bruin Walk. It's held at the beginning of each semester, and all the clubs and groups set up tents and tables down the main street of campus to recruit students to join. One semester I was walking down the corridor with some friends and I felt eyes tracking me as we walked from table to table. This isn't a new experience for me—I'm used to drawing attention and entertaining the stares of strangers. But this stranger was different. This guy was totally creeping me out.

Like I knew he would, he finally called out to me. "Hey, hey you!"

I sighed. "Yes?"

He and three other members of his team more or less cornered me. "Do you believe in God?" one asked.

That's not what I expected him to say. I glanced up at the

signage over their table. He was representing the coalition of campus atheists.

"Yes," I responded. "I do."

"But we can see you have a prosthetic," he argued. And I already knew where he was going.

Thanks for stating the obvious, I wanted to say, but held my tongue to reply, "Yup. I lost my leg when I was young."

"Don't you think if God were real, if there were a good, benevolent God, that you would have both legs right now?"

What I really wanted to point out to this dude was that suffering is an intrinsic piece of the human experience. That if he had actually read the Bible, he'd see that there was a tremendous amount of suffering when Jesus walked the earth.

But I realized very quickly that these were not the guys to go to war with. It would have been a waste of valuable time and energy. It's not like anything I could have said would have changed their minds. I think I just rolled my eyes and walked away, but that interaction is just another example of how people have used their religion—or lack of religion—to manipulate others in order to get what they want from them.

That day was an awakening moment for me. I decided right then and there that I was not going to impose my religion on anyone. I hated when somebody did that to me, so I refused to do that to someone else.

I think that's part of why I didn't end up getting into politics. Because on one hand, I feel I am a person of deep faith. But on the other hand, I don't believe my religion or my faith should dictate how other people choose to live their lives. I can only worry about one person's behavior—Scout's. And trust me—she's a handful.

DISCOVERING MY WHY

So, if I didn't want to go into politics, what was I going to do with my life?

Let's rewind a bit. Remember when I mentioned meeting Stan? That meeting with Stan would eventually change my entire life—and it would redefine my why.

About two years after meeting Stan, I received my first custom-made running prosthetic. But there was just one problem—I couldn't use a cosmetic cover over a running blade. I didn't want to stand out. I didn't want to be noticeable. I remember thinking, *If I can't cover this running blade, then I just won't run.* I was devastated, to be honest. I guess I hadn't considered all the possibilities when I asked for a limb that would allow me to be active.

The same day Stan gave me the running limb, he convinced me to run in a race there in Orlando—like, that night! But when I got to the track, I had something like an emotional breakdown. I started crying and I just couldn't stop. So there I was with this brand-new prosthetic, ugly-crying on the track.

"Don't make me do this," I wailed. But no one came to my rescue. Which was the best thing that could have happened to me.

This isn't where I tell you that I had some miraculous showing where, despite my misgivings, I was a total natural who came from behind to defeat the veteran runners. Homegirl came in dead last. Like, the girls who finished before me had already gotten out of the post-race shower. Just kidding—but I did lose pretty badly. But it didn't matter. As soon as I lined up on the track, I had already won. Because while I was running, I felt something I had never felt before: unlimited.

I felt this freedom. I felt that all the chains that had weighed me down for the last fourteen years had been lifted. When I was running, it felt like everything was going to be okay. It's an indescribable feeling, and the memory of it gives me chills even as I write this. I knew as I crossed the finish line that running had just become something I couldn't *not* do.

I think that's where we all have to start with our *why*. Especially as it informs the choices we make in terms of our career. You're going to spend one-third of your life at work. One-third. For me, that number is actually a little higher, but for the average American, one-third of all your time on this planet will be spent working a job. Obviously, you want to choose a career path you're passionate about—or at least that you can create passion about. You want to invest this one-third into something that makes you feel like I did that day on the track: unlimited.

You have no idea how many messages I get from girls on Instagram saying, "Scout, I feel stuck. I don't know what to do with my life. I'm working a dead-end job. It just feels empty. How did you know what you wanted to do with your life?"

The truth is, I didn't. Remember the story of the medical device sales gig? While that was a great opportunity, and I did well at it, it wasn't fulfilling. I always felt...like an impostor. Like I was playing the role of a sales rep, not that I was actually wired to be one. Maybe I knew all along that I was created to be a professional athlete. I see evidence of that when I look back on how I felt even as a kid. When I was telling people in school, "I'm going to do something great with my life. I don't know exactly what it is. But I will be great."

The kids I went to school with didn't necessarily go to big universities. They mainly went to a junior college and got an associate's degree, but no one went far from home. Scout Bassett—the already peculiar Asian with a disability—announced she was going to go to a prestigious university far away. Not only that, but I predicted I'd also get a full scholarship.

It was the equivalent of me saying I was going to become president one day or that I was going to make it to the NBA. I remember people looking at me like, *Good luck with that, honey.* All I know is that the dreams I've had for myself have always been different. And they were met with a lot of doubt, a lot of questions, and a lot of disdain from people around me. Even my own family, to a certain degree.

I think when you come from a background where there's been so much suffering and so much struggle and loss and pain, there's a part of you that feels like all of it is going to have meaning one day. All of it is going to be used for good. There's a verse in the Bible I love that talks about this idea—this idea of redemption: "And we know that in all things God works for the good of those who love him, who have been called according to his purpose" (Romans 8:28 NIV).

I imagine the root of my belief stems from this—because logically, my dreams for myself made no sense outside of God's plan for my life.

I had a pretty early sense of my purpose. What I mean by that is I didn't always know what my purpose was, but I grew up being taught that I had one—a unique one. I still believe that. I believe we all have a specific purpose. For a while when I was younger, I didn't see how that purpose would ever be possible. When I got to the United States, my parents immediately placed me in kindergarten. The phrase "culture shock" doesn't cut it. It was more like culture *electrocution*. I didn't know English. I had never read a book. I didn't even have context for what "school" meant.

I spent most of those early years feeling like I was always operating out of a deficit—like I was always coming from behind, playing catch-up. But as I began to acclimate—as much as one can acclimate under those circumstances—I slowly started to perform better at school. I stopped screaming every time my parents drove me somewhere—convinced they were taking me back to the orphanage. I started to trust. Not just trust the people around me, but trust myself, too. I dared to believe that what my parents and what the pastor said was true: My life had value. I had a purpose. I had to, right? How else does an eight-year-old kid with one leg get adopted outside of God's intervention?

I think it was around fifth grade when I realized that not only did I have a purpose but my purpose was going to be different. I had been set apart. Set apart to suffer, but set apart to succeed as well. And when your purpose is different, even if you don't know exactly what it is, your path may not look like the traditional path.

But for you, you may be wrestling with your purpose—with your why. You may not know exactly what it is you want to do, but you know you want it to be great. Maybe you're in college and maybe you're already well into a career field that you know isn't exactly what you've been wired to do. If you're struggling with your why, you're not alone. I just searched for books on purpose and Amazon lists 151,928 books on helping people figure out their purpose. That's a lot.

And I'm not sure what I can add to the conversation outside of my own experience, but one way I was able to identify my purpose was by knowing what I was good at. I think a lot of people give this advice, right? They'll say, "What do people compliment you on? What comes easily to you that doesn't necessarily come easily to other people?"

I think both of those questions are a great place to start. But I'd take it a step further. Ask yourself these questions:

1. What makes me feel unlimited?
2. What moves my heart?
3. What is something I always have energy for?

Whenever I step on the track, I get the same rush of adrenaline I did that day almost twenty years ago. I feel powerful. My heart is quiet. And I know I'm doing *exactly* what I was created by God to do.

But it's not just about the running. It's also about influence. About a platform. About using the voice sports has given me to do something bigger. See, people view athletes as entertainers. We're here to set records and win medals. But that's never been my goal in running. Sure, I like to win. I love to win, actually. But winning would be empty if that's all this sport was about for me. That's true for any job. If there's not a bigger why, none of the accolades, money, or attention will be enough to fulfill you long term.

BACK TO NANJING

After the Rio Games in 2016, I went back to the orphanage I lived in for the first eight years of my life. I already wasn't in a good place. After placing a disappointing fifth in the hundred meters and tenth in the long jump, the shadows of disappointment had already darkened my heart. I thought a trip back to the orphanage might be exactly what I needed to refocus and reprioritize. I was right—it just didn't go down the way I thought it would.

Twenty years later, not much had changed since I'd last been there. The kids still didn't receive any formal schooling, though there was an "entertainment teacher" who came in to do crafts with them. There was the same pervasive darkness in that place. The same sense of oppression and sadness. I wasn't allowed to go into certain areas of the building. I assume because those were the rooms the kids were "doing chores" in. Read: forced child labor. That thought still haunts me to this day.

The experience was so profound and so healing in many ways—to be able to go back and to love on those children, to feed babies, to color with toddlers, and to have a message of love and hope for them. To show them that they can make it out—not just alive, but alive and well. It was an incredible honor I didn't feel worthy of.

And at the same time, revisiting those memories was also incredibly painful. As soon as I walked inside, the stench of poverty and overcooked rice and sour urine fell across me like a wet blanket pressed to my face. I couldn't breathe. As I looked into the faces of those kids—starved in every way—I began to think of my biological parents, and of the guilt and shame they must have experienced because they couldn't take care of me. I'd never thought much about them until that visit. I'd certainly never wanted to find them. But after leaving Nanjing, it's really all I could think about. I wanted to show them: *Hey, I made it. I'm okay. I'm better than okay.* But more than that, I wanted them to know that I forgave them.

I didn't allow myself to cry until I got back home in the States. And once I started, I couldn't stop. In the weeks and months that followed, I went through a really dark place of not being okay. I kept having panic attacks and not being able to sleep. One whiff of that smell and suddenly I was right back where I was as a young girl.

One thing I haven't discussed a lot publicly is the child labor we were forced to endure as part of our stay in the orphanage. "Earning our keep," I guess is how the state viewed it. But it was abusive and gross and I still have a difficult time wrapping my mind around the rationale that, because our parents couldn't care for us or passed away, we had to work to stay barely alive. I obviously had unprocessed trauma and emotions from my stay in Nanjing that bubbled back to the surface with a vengeance that day.

I spent the next two years struggling. I hadn't realized how much of my past I was carrying around with me, lugging it over my shoulder like a sack full of dirty laundry. I hadn't realized how much joy my past was still sucking out of my life, either. I had a friend tell me, "Scout, your past doesn't need you. But your future does." Her words were a wake-up call to me to reach out to get help. I spent many, many hours in therapy working through the experiences that still had a hold on me.

I'd say this, too, about your why: You can't live out your *why* for today while you've still got one foot in the past. You have to step forward into the right now. If that takes forgiving someone, forgive them. If that takes letting go of disappointments, let them go. If that means leaving a toxic relationship, leave it. But I'm telling you—you'll never find the fulfillment of living out your why today if you haven't dealt with the *why me?* of yesterday.

My trip to Nanjing was a great reminder that we all have a choice in how we process our own history. No matter what's happened to you, even if it wasn't your fault, you have a choice in what you're going to do with that and whether or not you want to stay parked there, or if you want to become whole and to heal.

"But Scout," you might say, "you don't know what I've been through. You don't know what was done to me. You don't know what I've done."

That might be true, but I am a living testimony that a limited past can't hold you back from an unlimited future unless you give it permission to. *You* are the only person holding you back. Because listen, there have been times when I thought I was so damaged and broken and traumatized, that the scars were so big and deep, I didn't think wholeness was really achievable. But if you're willing to do the hard work, wholeness is not only achievable, it's guaranteed.

THE BIGGER WHY

One of the beautiful outcomes of my trip to Nanjing is that it spurred me to increase my advocacy and mentorship programs. I do a lot of work with the Challenged Athletes Foundation (CAF), which is the same foundation that paid for me to receive my first running prosthetic. I meet disabled athletes from all over the country and I have the genuine honor of showing them that being disabled doesn't make you less than or incapable.

Some of these kids, you guys. They're *young*. And they're navigating life without a limb—some from congenital defects and some from accidents—in a much different era than I did. I feel like there's so much more pressure on today's kids, even from an early age. The kids I get to serve through CAF need someone who is ahead of them to show them that, hey, you can still have a full, big, amazing life with a disability. You can even be a professional athlete.

I also see myself as a voice for both female athletes and minority athletes. I recently just finished a press tour celebrating the fiftieth anniversary of Title IX—the federal civil rights law that prohibits sex-based discrimination in a school or other program that receives federal funding.

Seeing that I can be an advocate for change, for equality, for inclusion has really helped me carve out my bigger why. And realizing that this work is so much more important than how many medals I've won or how many records I have has helped me get free from smaller whys.

Your bigger why is your legacy stuff. That's the stuff people talk about at your funeral. That's the stuff that goes on living long after you're gone. That's the stuff that brings you peace, brings you fulfillment.

And I feel like *this* is my bigger why. It's why God gave me this platform. It's why God allowed me to suffer. It's why God created Scout Bassett to begin with—to be a voice for those without a voice and to be an example of someone who broke through the ceiling for minorities, disabled persons, and women and made it to the top.

What is your legacy stuff? What is your bigger why? What cause do you believe in? Who can you come alongside? Someone you're just farther down the road from? Maybe it's as simple as mentoring a girl whose parents are getting divorced because you're from a divorced family. Or maybe you want to become an advocate for a bigger cause. You want to raise money to fight breast cancer. You want to raise awareness of childhood cystic fibrosis.

What cause can you further that doesn't further your cause? When you find the answer to that question, you've found your bigger why. And that's the why that will bring you the greatest satisfaction. Not just now, but for the rest of your life.

One person I really admire who has found a bigger why is a friend of mine named Allyson Felix. You may have heard of her—she's the most decorated US track-and-field athlete in Olympic history. She has eleven Olympic medals—more than any male track-and-field athlete, including Usain Bolt. She's ran the 200 meters, 400 meters, 100 meters, the 4x100-meter relay, and the 4x400-meter relay. She started her career at age seventeen in the 2003 national championships. Now, a mother at age thirty-five, Allyson is competing in some of the last races of her career. To say Allyson is a phenom would be an understatement.

But what I admire most about Allyson is the shift she's made in recent years to use her platform to advocate for Black women's maternal health, making sure they have financial support to pay for childcare while competing.

"I felt like I had to win all the medals, do all the things, before I could even think about starting a family, and that's something that I don't want my daughter to feel," she told NPR's *Morning Edition*.[1]

After Allyson was diagnosed with preeclampsia—a condition that could have been fatal—she had to have an emergency C-section. The track-and-field community were silent, which is pretty much how they treat every pregnancy. She wasn't afforded maternity leave and she feared contract cancellation if she didn't return to work quickly—in other words, prematurely. Her experience is not an exception. Athletes have been known to hide their pregnancies just to keep their sponsorships. How sad is that? Something that should be one of the biggest reasons to celebrate publicly becomes a "shameful" secret you have to conceal in order to pay the bills?

In addition to advocating for new mothers, Allyson is also working to provide childcare for female athletes. For mothers, one of the greatest obstacles to competing at the elite level is the cost of childcare while training and competing. Allyson is partnering with sponsors to grant childcare stipends of $10,000 to help moms pay for someone to watch the ones they love while they do what they love.

Finally, Allyson is supporting women through her sneaker brand Saysh. If a woman buys a pair of Saysh shoes and her foot grows in pregnancy, she can exchange her shoes for a brand-new, larger pair at no cost.

Allyson's difficult experience led her to her bigger why. I love it when people can take a bad situation and leverage it for good. That may be a place for you to start, too, when it comes to your bigger why. What's a wound or painful situation you've been in that you can use as a springboard for advocacy? How can you leverage your difficult situation for good?

MORE THAN AN OUTCOME

Allyson has been a great role model for me as I've gotten older in my career. She is the person who helped me to see I'm so much more than just an athlete, and I can be so much more than just an athlete. And as an athlete, I used to tell myself, *You're only as good as your last win or your latest result—that's the value you bring. And if you're not winning, you're not valuable.*

Allyson was able to change the narrative of who she is—that she's more than an athlete. She's an advocate, she's a fighter for women's rights. She's an entrepreneur, she's a trailblazer. And, oh, she also happens to be a really good athlete. Watching her, I started seeing my own career through a different lens. I realized I don't have to be reduced to a single label—to what I do for a living.

As an athlete, defining yourself by your last performance

is too much weight to carry. Nobody can live in that context because there's so much failure that happens in sports. So if outcomes are the measure, and you allow the public pressure and the expectations to perform and entertain to define you, it's a horrible way to live. I'm more than my wins. I'm more than my losses. And Allyson set that example for me to follow.

You saw this realization play out in real time with Simone Biles at the Tokyo 2020 Olympics. She posted on Twitter, "I'm more than my accomplishments and gymnastics which I never truly believed before."[2] You also saw it when Naomi Osaka withdrew from the French Open and then Wimbledon in 2021 after she was fined $15,000 for refusing to speak to the press at the French Open. Her team announced she was taking time off to spend with friends and family. Instead of competing at the top of her game, Osaka chose to prioritize her mental health. I applaud both her and Biles for coming to the realization that we are so much more than an outcome.

The idea that I'm more than an outcome was reinforced after the disappointment of not making the 2020 Paralympic team in Tokyo. Because I wasn't competing, I was asked by NBC Sports to cover the games as a news correspondent. Which, to me, felt very important. Rarely do you see Asians in the space of broadcast journalism and even more uncommon are people with disabilities. To be able to represent both groups of intersectionality was an exciting opportunity even though I wasn't running in the Games.

Tokyo taught me that one Games, one trial, one injury—those things don't define me. What really defines me is how responsible I am with the opportunities God brings me. How I react to disappointment. How I use my platform to elevate others.

Even if you're not an athlete, it can be difficult not to be defined by your performance. If your why is attached to your achievement, you're always going to be in this cycle of affirmation-seeking that is exhausting and not at all fulfilling. Instead of asking, "What do I do?" ask, "Who am I?" Because you can be laid off from a job, you can be rejected by someone you care about, you can lose out on a chance to appear at the Paralympics, but you can't ever be separated from your purpose. Your purpose endures.

I think I turned a corner with this mindset when I began investing more in the athletes I mentor. Whether I win or lose isn't going to change their lives. My outcomes and my performance are not going to affect their future, but if I can take the opportunities that I have—the platforms I have—to speak up about issues that they're dealing with, I have the chance to build something meaningful and lasting. It's going to be a difference-maker for them. *That's* worth celebrating way more than a number on a timer.

But if we don't have our identity firmly rooted in a foundation that's beyond our achievement, you will find yourself striving and inevitably failing, living and longing for something more. The biggest win in life has nothing to do with medals.

The biggest win in life is figuring out your why, and having the courage to live out the answer.

One last thing—it's natural to get discouraged when you're discovering your why. There's an emotional dip that can occur and it can make you feel like you're doing life "wrong" or that you're the only one who doesn't have it together. The only way out is to keep pushing—to keep exploring your gifts and talents and interests. And to remember that you're more than an outcome.

Finding your own purpose—your why—may take time, but it will unlock the door to an unlimited future that's more fulfilling and life-giving than you could ever imagine.

CHAPTER SEVEN

THE COMEBACK

Twenty-six.

That was the number of spots Team USA was allowed to bring to the 2020 Paralympic Games in Tokyo. Twenty-six. Do you know where I sat on the list?

Twenty-eight.

It was a miracle I'd even made it to trials, which is the competition you participate in to qualify for the Paralympics. In the months leading up to Tokyo—in the COVID-19 "extra year"—I started having acute foot pain. It felt like I was running on knives. Since I'm missing the big toe on my left side, when I run, I put an intense amount of stress on my foot, and that stress caused problems in my foot. I underwent an unexpected surgery, which derailed my training and made standing at the starting line of trials feel out of reach. In fact, a week out from the event, we still weren't sure I'd make it there.

Despite the hell I'd been through in 2020, I made it to trials and even had a season's high in the long jump and 100 meters. I hadn't put up my best numbers, but they weren't my worst numbers, either. I knew I was going to be right around the Team USA contention threshold. So then...we waited. And waited. And waited.

See, there's a selection process in the Paralympics that involves taking a limited number of athletes to the Games—the decision committee picks the athletes whom they think have the best chance of winning. Each country gets a certain number of athlete "slots," and the committee chooses who gets to go. We'll come back to the selection process later, but for now know that it feels like one of the most discriminatory aspects of being a female Paralympic athlete. Because guess who gets most of the slots: men.

Seven days I waited as my career, my reputation, my sponsorships, my livelihood, my *life* hung in the balance. Then the word came down. I hadn't been chosen and I was *two spots* away from competing. I had been named an alternate.

Disappointment *flooded* through me. I thought I might drown in it. There was the sting of humiliation, too. But mostly? It was so freaking painful. To this day, when I think back to when I learned I wasn't competing in Tokyo, I still get nauseated. It was soul-crushing heartache.

This dream of mine shattered into a million little pieces and I felt each and every one break apart inside of me. Five years. *Five years* of my life dedicated to a moment and I just wasn't healthy enough to pull it off. If we'd competed when we were supposed to in 2020, I would have crushed it. But what-ifs don't earn gold medals. Great performances do. And mine was good—but it wasn't great.

In the days and weeks that followed, I was not okay. For someone who is typically emotionally mild, it was an alien experience—having *all* the feelings *all* the time. I started waking up in the middle of the night with panic attacks. Fear had such a grip on me my throat would feel like it was closing and I couldn't draw in enough air.

Will I ever run again? I worried. *Am I done? Is my story over? Where do we go from here?*

It took quite some time before I stabilized. This wasn't just a race disappointment. This was a career disappointment. A brand disappointment. A sponsor disappointment. Not appearing in Tokyo wasn't just bad for my pride, it was bad for business. That's part of what gives being a professional athlete such added pressure. You do have an expiration date. At some point you will slow down. You just hope you aren't the last one to realize that your time is up.

At thirty-three years old, I know many people expected me to retire. My body was tired, but my spirit was not. In fact, not making the 2020 Games set my determination on fire. Though

I was proud of the grit and courage I showed to make it to trials, I knew God wasn't done with my story as a professional athlete.

So I went back to work. I made some big changes, including a change in coaching.

So often in our lives, when something isn't working—maybe it's a job, a relationship, or a dynamic of our routine—when we're not getting the results we want, we become paralyzed. We just sit in it. Because change is scarier than the familiar even though the familiar isn't great. And before we know it, time has passed and we're still in the same place we've always been in.

I had been with my previous coach for seven years, the last three of which were not great for either of us. It was time to move on, but I was scared. One thing I've learned is that the moment you think you need to make a change, you've already needed to make that change for quite some time. But the idea of starting over is daunting, right? And for me, going into the eleventh year of my career, starting over almost felt silly. But I had a choice: Stay the same or take a chance.

I wasn't willing to miss out on an opportunity to get better, so I started putting out feelers for coaches. It was terrifying, to be honest. It's a struggle for para-athletes to find coaches who are interested in working with us. And this search was no exception. I called a lot of people and the response was the same: "I don't do para-athletes," which often means, *I don't do charity cases.* Because they see working with disabled athletes as a step down from working with able-bodied or NCAA athletes.

So I didn't have a lot of options. I heard so many noes in the process that I almost became immune to the word. Ultimately, two coaches were interested, and I ended up going with my gut and hiring a two-time Olympian out of San Diego State University.

The first nine months of our partnership I was worried. I thought, *Did I make the right move? Was this the right decision?* Because it was all so new. This coach had a different style and new ways of doing things, which made me feel uncomfortable. It was rough. In fact, we didn't start to find our groove—our lightning in a bottle—until we'd been working together for two years. That's a long time to feel uncertain about a decision, but I had to choose to trust the process.

That's the first lesson I learned on making a comeback—you have to make some changes. And often, those changes will be both uncomfortable and scary.

Because I'm a professional athlete, my schedule is very structured. For the most part, my days look the same. I had to recognize that *especially* under those circumstances, change of any kind is hard, and that to move lanes so drastically would naturally bring with it some growing pains. But I won't lie—I was terrified I'd made the wrong pivot.

"Pivot" is an important word when it comes to lessons on making a comeback. It's actually one of my favorite words in the English language. There's a podcast called *The Pivot* I love because it's so practical. It showcases stories about people who are successful and who thrive because they are willing to make a pivot.

A pivot simply means you're willing to go a different direction. You're willing to make changes. You're willing to try new things in order to get where you want to be. People who pivot are people who don't get stuck. You don't reach an obstacle and say, "Well, I guess I'm going to give up now." No, you pause, acknowledge the obstacle, but then you pivot directions, methods, or applications and you keep going.

Sometimes these pivots are forced on you. Sometimes you choose to pivot. But if you want to make a comeback, you've got to learn how to pivot, which requires two skills:

1. **Humility.** Being able to admit that the direction you were going isn't working is essential to being able to pivot. If you dig your heels in stubbornly and keep doing the same things that aren't working, you're never going to get better and your life will not improve. But if you can release control and entertain new ideas and ways of doing things? You'll be able to pivot.

2. **Resiliency.** The first half of pivoting is realizing you're going the wrong direction. The second half is deciding to take action, to do something—and to keep working at it. Resilient people don't give up. They understand that if you want to achieve, if you want to succeed, it might take more than one try. In

fact, it's highly likely that you're going to have to try and fail over and over again. But as long as you continue to pivot, you still have a shot at your dreams.

COMEBACK KID

When I first started with my new coach, I was not running very well. The first two months of the season were spent in anxiety. *Oh my gosh,* I thought, *I've just completely upended my life, reinvented myself, and put in a lot of effort to pivot just to have the same results—if not, worse results.*

I remember having this conversation with my coach when we were running in the mid to low seventeen seconds, which is about average. Not podium numbers at all. I said to her, "Are we okay? Should I be worried?"

"This is no time to panic," she said. "You're fine. By Nationals, you're going to be exactly where you want to be." She told me to trust the plan and the process.

So that's what I did. I showed up every day and I chose to trust that at some point, the hard work would pay off. That's where discipline comes into play. To me, discipline is doing the next right thing over and over again until you see results. This same principle applies to life, too—you've got to be willing to take incremental improvements. You can't expect to make a comeback overnight. That doesn't even happen in the movies. Comebacks take time. Discipline means you show up whether you want to or not, whether you feel like it or not, or whether you think it's worth it or not.

And you know what? Week by week, I started to see little improvements. They weren't grand or sweeping or dramatic. The improvements were very gradual. Every practice and every meet I began to gain ground—an inch at a time—but I was still gaining ground.

In your life, maybe instead of shedding seconds, you're shedding trauma in therapy. You don't have major breakthroughs at every appointment, but one day you wake up and you feel a little stronger. Or maybe you're shedding negativity. Every day you work to control your mind and thoughts a little more and a little more. Or you're shedding toxic relationships. You grow more and more disconnected from unhealthy people until they're no longer in your life. If you want to make a comeback, discipline is required.

As my times came down, my confidence grew. My self-belief grew. And then it was just cyclical. The more confident I grew, the better my times were. The better my times were, the more confident I grew. It was this beautiful rhythm of effort and results that I had only experienced before in 2017 when I won my first two global medals.

In June 2022, it was time for Nationals. Though I was a six-time National Champion, it had been four years since I'd won my last national title. But the insecurities I'd felt following Tokyo were nowhere in sight. I had done the next right thing over and over again. I'd pivoted and been disciplined. I'd done my part—whatever happened next, I'd done everything I could to prepare for.

I knew a couple of the girls I was competing against were capable of running fast times. But I just *knew* that I wouldn't be defeated. Of course, you're always nervous. But my nerves were electric. They were excitement. I was that confident.

Two nights before the race is actually the most important night of sleep you get in preparation for a meet. It's assumed that nobody's getting any sleep the night before. The nerves, the anxiety, the excitement—chemically, it's almost impossible for your brain to allow you to sleep. So two nights out you really want to make sure you're getting good, quality rest.

Two nights out I got in bed before the sun went down. Typically, this is when my mind starts running its own race. I run through the meet over and over again in my mind, playing out all the scenarios of what it will take for me to win. But that night, I had this almost odd sense of peace. My mind was quiet. My spirit was still. I wasn't worried. I was ready. I knew we'd prepared. I knew the results had spoken for themselves. And as long as I showed up the same way I had been showing up at practice, I had no chance of losing.

When you're an athlete you never want to go into a major event thinking, *I have to have the performance of a lifetime to win this thing. To make the final. To be selected.* That's never a good place to be because more times than not, it doesn't happen. I knew I didn't have to do anything crazy. I just had to run the same race I'd been running in practice.

I think there's a lesson for us all here, and it's one of my favorite philosophies: Hope is not a strategy. Hope is not a plan. Hope is not a training method. Hope is not a skill. Now, don't hear me say that hope is not important. Hope is critical to joy. Hope is critical to progress. But hope alone isn't enough. Your responsibility in life is to put yourself in the best position possible so that hope isn't the only thing you're hanging on to.

Let me give you an example. Remember in school when you didn't study for that big exam and when the teacher passed out the tests and you started reading the questions all you could do was *hope* you were giving the right answers? That's what I'm talking about. Hope is a poor substitute for preparation. If you want something in life, work for it. Don't *just* hope for it.

When I got to the meet, there was an optional prelim race. I didn't really want to do it, but my coach encouraged me to run so I could get out any nerves. My biggest competitor whom I hadn't beat since 2019 ran in the prelims, too. I was like, okay. This is going down. If I can slay this dragon in the prelim, you can't tell me nothing about defeat in the finals. It wasn't even a close race between us. There was another girl who brought some heat, but I won the prelim handily.

Then it was time for the actual final. All the hard work, the sacrifice, the fears, and the triumphs culminated when I crossed the finish line at the 2022 US Nationals. I ran a personal best and I took home the title of National Champion.

All the weight of the last few years was lifted off my shoulders. All the noise and trash talking people had done about me was silenced when that gold medal was placed around my neck. I'd heard it all leading up to Nationals—that I was washed up, too old, needed to be done. Those narratives and criticisms became obsolete on that track that day.

That win said, "Hey. I'm back." And not just back, but I ran a personal best. I got better. Talk about a comeback.

There's nothing more gratifying than being able to execute what you want to do. It wasn't a perfect race, but there were some things that I did really well that I was proud of. And the other great thing I learned about myself from Nationals is that I can be clutch—I can be a gamer. I had struggled with that mental aspect of racing for the last few years, and it was like I finally regained the courage I needed to perform on a big stage—to come out swinging when my back is against the wall.

This is a skill I have developed in my personal life as well—the skill of being clutch. A "clutch" person is someone who is dependable. Who does what it takes to put themselves in the best position possible. Being clutch means you deliver under pressure. You're not afraid to try and you never, under any circumstances, give up.

What would being clutch look like in your life? Would it mean answering phone calls you'd rather avoid? Would it mean doing away with procrastination and doing the hard work on time, every time? Or would it mean weeding out some of the more challenging relationships in your life that drain you of time and energy? Sometimes the most clutch thing you can do is create boundaries and enforce them.

THE TRUTH OF THE COMEBACK

A lot of times, when we see people succeed, we only see the smiles and hear the applause. We don't see what happened in the middle. We don't see their journey. Those early days were dark. Had you told me that I would be winning a national title in 2022, I'm not sure I would have believed you. In fact, I probably would have done that weird laugh-cry thing where I was desperate to believe you, but also saw no evidence that your words could be true.

But the middle of the journey is the most important part of a comeback. It's usually ugly and hard, but that's where the magic happens. That's where the deposits are made. But to get there, you have to first come to a place of suffering. I know that sounds dramatic, but it's true. The way humans are wired is that we're not likely to make a change unless we experience a little suffering—a little pain. A little discomfort.

The very definition of comeback implies some sort of setback, right? They go hand in hand. You can't have a comeback without a setback. This is where your mental game becomes more important than ever. When we experience a setback, we've got to learn to reframe the experience as an opportunity to improve, to grow—to come back.

Lost your job? It's an opportunity to find a better one. Your friend group is leaving you out? It's an opportunity to find people who prioritize you. Going through a bad breakup? It's an opportunity to learn more about yourself and about what you really want and need from a partner.

If you find yourself in the middle of a setback right now, you're standing at a crossroads. You can either stay the same, staying where you are and sitting in the slop of regret, or you can dust yourself off and choose a new path. I found a new coach, a new training facility, and a new program. Maybe you need a new career path, a new passion, a new school, a new set of boundaries with friends and family.

One thing that I can tell you about comebacks is they almost always involve a reinvention of some part of yourself. Don't be afraid to take risks. They could be your stepping stone to coming back. Give yourself permission to change and evolve. The way you have always been isn't the way you have to stay. In fact, I'd go as far as to say if you aren't evolving in some area of your life regularly, you may be in a spiral of stagnancy.

You've heard that word before, right? *Stagnant.* Which basically means that you're unmoving. You're unchanging. You remain the same. But if you really dissect the meaning of stagnant as it's applied to water—its most typical use—a more graphic picture emerges.

Stagnant water is water that is left sitting still for a long period of time. Without movement, that water becomes toxic. It becomes a breeding ground for bacteria and disease. I'd say that's a fair metaphor for our own lives when we become stagnant for too long. If we aren't growing or changing, it's likely we're unhealthy. Not just ourselves, but to the people who love and care about us, too.

HOW TO MAKE A COMEBACK

I've experienced more setbacks than I can count. And I think one of the hardest parts of those seasons is that initial feeling of loss of control. When things are going my way, I feel like I'm in the driver's seat. I'm in charge. But when things don't go my way, I don't immediately know what to do. And I hate that feeling. The key moments in my own comebacks always happen when I take action, bringing the situation back into my hands, leading me to make the needed changes.

Turns out, there's some significant science behind the mindsets of people who comeback from setbacks. A 2014 study published by *Neuron* took an in-depth look at what happens in our brains when we encounter a setback.[1] Researchers had participants play a game where they encountered setbacks. During the game, researchers used magnetic resonance (fMRI) to scan the participants' brains while they played the game. After each setback, players would have to decide whether they were going to persist with their current path or if they were going to start over and try a new one.

The results of the study showed that when people believe they have control over their setbacks, specific parts of the brain are activated and they're able to keep pushing forward toward a comeback. On the other hand, the individuals in the study who felt the situation was beyond their control experienced increased activity in a different area of the brain in charge of deciding whether or not a person gives up.

One way to feel like you have control over your setbacks is to make a plan for overcoming them—to strategize. I don't know about you, but I'm a girl who likes a plan. I thrive on strategy. And when it comes to setbacks, we don't have to enter that race without a strategy. See, when I look back at my most challenging moments, I recognize them as setbacks that have prepared me for some of my greatest learning experiences—some of my greatest comebacks. In hindsight, I also see a pattern of thoughts and behaviors that have taken me from setback to comeback. If I were coaching you through a setback, here's how I would tell you to handle it:

1. Assess the damage.
You start off by assessing what's happened. What went wrong? What was your role in what went wrong? How far is this setback going to set you back?

I keep a daily journal where I record most of my day—my diet, my workouts, how I'm feeling physically and emotionally.

Looking back at those records has been an invaluable resource for troubleshooting why I'm experiencing a setback. I can say, "Oh, I haven't gotten a good night's sleep in a week. No wonder I snapped at the Starbucks barista." I'd encourage you to keep a journal, too. Maybe not daily, but at least weekly. Keep track of your thoughts and emotions. Keep track of how you're investing in yourself and others. You may see a setback coming before it even happens.

2. Pivot.

After you've assessed the setback, make a change. Don't stay stuck, sitting in the mess. And don't retreat! An integral aspect of comebacks is reinvention. Things don't change if things don't change. Maybe it's an attitude change. A relationship change. Or a positive habit you need to rotate into your routine.

One of the coolest things about making positive changes in one aspect of your life is that it trickles down to benefit other parts of your life as well. You'll begin to view yourself, God, and others in a different way. When I moved from LA to San Diego to train, it touched every part of my life. Not only did that change bring a new coach, but it also brought new training techniques and recovery methods. I've also made new friends, traveled to new places, and regained my confidence in the context of a new setting.

Don't rationalize immobility and don't make excuses. Just make the needed changes and push off that pivot foot and go.

3. Let it go.

We all need a do-over every now and then. That's not only normal, it's human. So when you go through a setback—when you mess up or someone does you wrong—you will never make a comeback unless you learn how to simply let it go.

Following the Tokyo Games, I was devastated. But as a professional athlete, loss is just part of the job. I've wallowed in defeat in the past, but this time I determined not to allow that loss to derail my future win. I took off training for a month and traveled the world. With each mile I traveled, I let go a little more and a little more. By the time I got back home, I was ready to get back to work. And that's what I did. I released regret, I released rejection, and I released the embarrassment of falling short. Now, I have a National Championship medal that reminds me of the power of letting go.

For you, letting go may be fully internal. It may be something you need to work out through prayer or mediation. Maybe you need to have a difficult conversation to let go. Maybe you need to end a relationship. Whatever it is that is tying you to your past, sever it. Don't let regret anchor you to the shore. Cut ties and push out into the waters of new possibilities.

4. Reenter reality.

Something interesting that happens when we have setbacks is that we enter something I call survival mode. We sort of withdraw and turn inward, licking our wounds and rehearsing our pain. That's fine for a season—it's grieving. But there comes a time when you have to come back into the real world and engage again. Otherwise, your setback begins to take on a larger-than-life quality and it begins to define you. Soon, all you can think about and all you can talk about is your setback. You'll grow bitter, stay stagnant, and alienate the people who care about you.

Survival mode is not how we were created to live. It's an incredibly limiting mindset that stunts your growth and holds you back. One way I've made myself "reenter" reality is to put a timer on how long I'm going to let something rule my mind.

A friend of mine was going through a tough breakup. She would not stop talking about this dude, and he was long gone. There was no hint that reconciliation was on the horizon for them. And yet, it was like a broken record every time we talked or hung out. Finally I just said, "Look, you're gonna have to circle a date on the calendar. Whether it's today, tomorrow, or ninety days from now. Circle a date for when this guy isn't going to rule your conversations any longer."

And you know what? She did. She circled a date. And she stopped talking about him. Sometimes, you have to circle a date and move on. Think and talk about something different. Reenter reality on reality's terms.

5. Make your comeback.

In 2022, my comeback meant getting a gold medal. But other times coming back has simply meant I dared to dream again. I dared to set new goals. I dared to try. I dared to show my face in public. I dared to line up on the track again. Not every comeback looks like a miracle on the outside, but they are just that—little miracles that reset our lives and refresh our souls.

It's hard for all of us to recover from a loss. Career-wise, parenting-wise, relationship-wise.

We automatically go to I'm-a-failure mentality. I'm a failure because my marriage fell apart. I'm a failure because I didn't get that job or because I was laid off. I'm a failure because I yelled at my kids today. I'm a failure because I just saw all my friends together on social media and I didn't get the invite. It's so easy to reduce ourselves to those moments. It's so easy to say that our worth is lessened in the midst of a setback. I understand this mindset better than you know.

⸺ ⸺

It's been hard for me to wrap my mind around the idea that I'm more than what feels true in any given moment. I mean, it's especially hard because *so much* rides on how well I do on the track. My sponsorships, my future opportunities, my ability to maintain a platform to help others. So how can I *not* define myself based on my current condition?

I think it just comes down to choosing to see beyond your setbacks. To reminding yourself every day that you're capable of so much more than you think you are. That your value is inherent because you are a person created with a purpose. And that purpose extends beyond robotically getting it right every time. This realization has spurred me to speak out more. To talk about athletes' rights, human rights, equal pay, and equal opportunities. Because when you see that you're more, you're empowered to do more.

Play the movie of your life. Go ahead—rehearse those setbacks. Rehearse those losses and failures. Do it one last time. Now, I want you to think of a song that gets you pumped. You know the song—the one you turn up to warp volume in the car when you're by yourself. You might as well be in Madison Square Garden when this song comes on, you perform it with conviction—like it's your own. Think of that song. Okay, now I want you to lay that track against this moment of your life. Because this is the part of the movie where you make your big comeback. This is the part of your ESPN *30 for 30* where the voiceover says, "But then things took a turn. She realized that she was more than a setback. She realized she had something important to do with her life. So she stood up, wiped her face, and she made a comeback."

Don't limit your future by letting your setback become a step back. Reframe setbacks as an opportunity to grow, to pivot, and to come back. The best stories are the stories of a comeback kid.

CHAPTER EIGHT

BUILDING YOUR TEAM

I was in an on-again, off-again relationship for over five years that almost derailed my entire career.

He didn't seem like a terrible guy when I met him, but we brought out the very worst in each other. Together, we were toxic. I'm talking *sludge*. I remember being at multiple events—championships, even—and being so drained, so emotionally exhausted, that I wasn't giving my best performance. He was a constant distraction. I knew it wasn't right, but I also didn't know how to get out of the unhealthy cycle.

Then something happened between us that couldn't be undone and I was finally able to walk away. But I didn't walk away unscathed. I had allowed the status of our relationship, the things he said, and his behavior to get in my head and keep me there. Looking back, I see how that relationship robbed me of important moments in my life—moments I can't get back.

I remember in particular being at a World Championship meet and waiting for my event to start and wishing I were anywhere—literally anywhere—other than where I was because my mental game was so off. Our relationship was like a roller coaster. Those highs were exhilarating—they'd take my breath away and I felt invincible. But then the lows took my stomach with them—leaving me rattled and shaky and shell-shocked.

When I finally got sick and tired of being sick and tired, I was able to cut ties between the two of us. In the months and years that followed, I realized just how toxic that relationship had been for me. For both of us, I'm sure. That experience showed me how important it is to only surround yourself with people who are aligned with your goals, beliefs, and values. Because when someone isn't for what you're for, even if they're not outwardly against it, you will be pulled away from it.

Right now, my priorities are competing and advocacy. Anyone who doesn't further those two passions does not belong in my inner circle. They don't belong on my team.

WHAT'S A TEAM?

In sports, the term "team" can mean a couple of different things. Take the Braves, for example. They're a team with forty players on the roster. They rely on each other. They depend on each other. They have to trust each other and work together in order to pull out the big wins. This is the traditional definition of team.

For me, my team consists of a few different people. I have an agent, who manages my calendar, books appearances, and works with my sponsors. I have a coach, who trains and coaches me. I have a medical team I see regularly to make sure my body is in peak performance mode. I also have Stan—the first doctor to ever give me a prosthetic—who still advises on and adjusts my prosthetics. My team are the people I work closely with but also those who walk with me through my life, my closest friends. My team are the people I listen to, the people I seek feedback from, and the people I allow to shape my decisions and life.

What does a team look like for you?

You may not realize it, but you already have a team. Your team is the people you listen to, the people you seek feedback from, and the people you allow to shape your decisions and life. Your team is your friends, the people you look up to, and anyone who has influence over you. And if you're not being intentional with how you build your team, chances are, your team could be doing you more harm than good.

Have you ever driven a car with tires that are out of alignment? I learned how to drive on a car that you had to steer toward the right just to make it go straight. The steering wheel shook the entire time. It was totally drivable, but it wasn't safe.

That's how our lives are when we have toxic or unhealthy teammates or friends. These relationships cause us nagging issues, annoyance, and sometimes pain. These relationships limit us, but we aren't able to pinpoint the exact source of all these negative consequences.

BAD CALLS

I haven't always chosen the best people to be in my inner circle. Take an agent I had at one time, for example. Working with her felt like working with a complete con artist. Since representing me, she's endured some legal repercussions for professional misconduct. So why did I sign with someone that shady? Honestly, it was two factors: inexperience and desperation.

The warning signs were pretty apparent from the very beginning. But I didn't have anyone else looking to represent me. Nobody else was knocking on my door. I didn't have a single commercial contract at the time or a sponsor or an offer. So the idea that this woman wanted to be my agent *and* she already had a sponsor on the table? To me, it was a no-brainer.

One thing I always tell my mentees now is that if someone offers to represent them who is offering the sun, the moon, and the stars, and it sounds too good to be true, it probably is.

Something I love about my current agent is that she is incredibly realistic. She'll say, "Scout, here's where we're at. No more, no less." She's very direct, and precise, and logical. In 2018, when I hit a low point in my career, she didn't sugarcoat a *thing* for your girl. She was like, "This is the number of partners you can expect to have as sponsors. But I'm not guaranteeing you they will commit. I'm not going to get your hopes up that it's going to be beyond that number, either."

One thing to look for in someone you want on your team is a person who isn't afraid to tell you hard truths. It does you no good for someone to tell you only what you want to hear. Of course, you want teammates who are positive and speak life-giving words, too. But you don't want teammates who lie to you because it's easier. People who surround themselves with ego-massagers are like people who live off candy as a diet. Too much sugar will make you sick and ineffective.

But Lindsay also offers hope. She said, "But I think we can be strategic with your partners. This is how I think we can move the needle. This is how we can build and you can continue to earn a living. It's tough right now, but this is where you're at."

Other people I interviewed filled me with crap and promised me things I knew they couldn't deliver on. "I can make you a star! I can get you this cover! I can get you that appearance! I can get you this sponsor!"

You don't want people on your team who can't be honest with you. In the end, it'll be *you* who suffers for it—not them.

Moving from my first agent to Lindsay taught me an incredibly valuable lesson: Pay less attention to what people say and pay more attention to what people do.

This is where you have to take a step back and assess someone's history. For me, that means doing background checks and checking references. But for you, it could simply mean you pay attention. If you are friends with someone who has left a trail of broken relationships in their wake, beware. If they're constantly blaming other people, if they always have trouble getting along with coworkers, if they're the common denominator in every negative interaction...they may not be the team member for you.

You want to look at consistency. You want to look at follow-through. You want to look for someone who does what they say they're going to do. For athletes, this is incredibly important. When you're starting out and you're not making any money, you can make decisions that you deeply regret later. The same is true for friendships made out of desperation. Out of loneliness. If you're settling for just any teammate, it's likely you'll pay some consequences for it later.

Another area that can get incredibly sticky is your relationship with your family. I want to honor my own family, but I will say that it hasn't always been easy. When you experience a modicum of success, you may have family members come out of the woodwork looking for a come-up. And you're like, "Um, who are you again? The second cousin of my third cousin on my mom's side? Are we even really related, then?" You will experience people who feel like you owe them part of your success, even if they had absolutely nothing to do with it.

This is where you have to have boundaries. This is when the word "no" becomes the most powerful word in the English language for you. Sure, you may get some passive-aggressive things posted about your "ingratitude" or "self-importance" on Facebook like I did, but at the end of the day, you owe nothing to anyone but *you*.

THE FRIEND-MANCE

You can get therapy for pretty much any relationship dynamic...except friendships. Think about it. There's couples therapy. There's sex therapy. There's individual therapy. There's family therapy. There's marriage therapy. You can even get workplace therapy and coaching to teach you how to have healthy interactions with your coworkers or become a better leader. But there is no such thing as friendship therapy. Which is odd, right? Think about it. Friendships are some of the most important—if not *the* most important—relationships we'll enjoy during our lifetime. And yet, there's not a lot of cultural importance placed on how to be a good friend or how to find a good friend.

I had a friend once we'll call Yael. As a professional athlete, I don't have a lot of margin to invest in meaningful friendships. That's what made my relationship with Yael so special. She was a physical trainer in one of the gyms I worked out in regularly. As part of my work, I got to hang out with Yael.

Our friendship started off intensely. And people don't talk about this enough, but we had a total friend-mance. When there's a friend-mance, there's a certain level of chemistry. You just *get* each other. You're on the same wavelength. You don't have to explain yourself because they understand you. You look forward to their texts—not unlike how you look forward to the texts of someone you have a romantic crush on—but this isn't that. Friend-mances feel safer because there aren't romantic feelings involved. But don't be mistaken—there are certainly *feelings*.

The minute Yael and I exchanged numbers, we were texting like crazy. We had the same sense of humor—dry and sarcastic. We held the same political beliefs, the same values. We were both raised as minorities in predominately white areas. We both had lost touch with our families. We both had had spiritual shifts, where our faiths had sort of transformed into something more personal and real—into something that aligned with our own convictions and experiences. We talked all day, every single day.

Then there was a shift. About a year into our friendship, Yael started talking about her *other* best friend all the time. At first, I was like, *That's great. I travel all the time, so I can't really do a lot of girls' nights out. It's good she has someone to spend time with.* But over time, her comments felt more like intentional jabs. Like she was passive-aggressively letting me know this new best friend was superior to me.

Then there were the criticisms. These, again, came indirectly. "I don't see how you're so okay not having a life," she said about my training schedule. "Personally, I couldn't sacrifice *everything* for any career. Don't you get lonely? I'd get lonely. Always by myself. I worry about you, Scout. Are you sure you're doing okay? All these competitions and meets can't be good for your self-esteem. You have lost a lot lately, right? Maybe it's time to set some new goals for yourself outside of sports."

The flags weren't just red. The flags had kerosene poured on them and had gone up in flames. No longer was my friendship with Yael life-giving or positive. No longer were our goals aligned. It was clear she was not *for* me, but for her version of me. But still, I couldn't let go of the friendship.

I'd defend myself, for sure. I'd explain why I'm so focused and determined. I'd reason out how I take care of my mental health on the road. I don't know why, but I felt obligated to help her understand something that no one besides me really needs to understand.

Then it got even more toxic. If I didn't tell Yael exactly what she wanted to hear, she started to leave me on "read" and send my calls to voicemail. I would get *so* mad, right? So then I'd ignore her. I would intentionally skip her stories on Instagram (tell me I'm not the only person who's done this to someone). And if she *did* text back, I'd make her wait hours before I'd send the deadliest text of all time from me: the thumbs-up emoji.

Sidebar: If you get the thumbs-up emoji from me, consider it a "shots fired" response.

Anyway, we went back and forth like this for a few months before one day she sent me a text that was at least three swipes long. You know when you see that huge blue box on the screen that something is about to either hurt your feelings or piss you off. Her words did both.

"Scout," she wrote, "I think it's time we just call this friendship. It's obvious that you are never going to change…"

This chick broke up with me. Over text! This person I'd shared my secrets with, my dreams with, my fears with—with a single text (more like a monologue), she cut me out of her life as if I were some sort of cancer. I'm not a person who gets sad. I typically express those kinds of emotions through anger or I don't express them at all. But this…this made me sad. Really sad. I felt rejected. I felt like there must be something wrong with me. From the outside, it looked like Yael had all these wonderful friends and I didn't. So I must be the problem, right?

WOUNDS

After the incident with Yael, I felt like I'd been wounded. I'd tell myself, *Somebody doesn't want to be friends with you anymore. So, what? You're a grown-up. Get over it.* But it still hurt and I didn't understand why.

I started journaling about the experience and sort of working out my feelings through writing. The more I wrote, the lighter I felt. Slowly, that wound began to heal until one day I was strong enough to look in the mirror and say, "Hey, Scout. You're worthy of love. You're worthy of friendship. So you know what? I'm going to be *your* best friend."

My reflection looked back at me like, *Yup. We've finally lost it,* but I tried to stay true to my words. I was determined to like myself. To be comfortable spending time alone. To not always crave the company (even text company) of someone as some sort of affirmation of my value. This happened to be at the very start of the global pandemic and lockdown, so I really had no choice. It was time to learn to like myself.

It sounds ridiculous, but I learned a lot about Scout Bassett during this season of isolation. I learned that I *don't* actually like true crime. It gives me anxiety and leaves me convinced someone's about to off me every time it gets dark. I confirmed my genuine affinity for all things sports. I could watch a Braves game from any season—the 1990s, early 2000s. It doesn't matter. I love watching competitors do what they love.

I realized I am more sensitive in the morning hours. Those are the times I felt the loneliest, and as the day progressed, I felt increasingly more comfortable in my own skin. I also learned I'm not great at being still. I guess I already knew that, but I was able to develop some strategies that allowed me to rest and refuel not just my body, but my soul as well.

Before you can expect to create a solid friendship with someone else, you've got to learn how to be a friend to yourself first. Heal the wounds of past failed relationships. Establish a firm foundation to build some meaningful and life-giving friendships in the future.

SIGNS A FRIENDSHIP NEEDS TO BE BENCHED (OR CUT FROM THE ROSTER)

It wasn't until years later that I was able to look back and see my friendship with Yael for what it really was—codependent and toxic. I'm no stranger to unhealthy relationships—I don't think any of us are. Humanity is inherently flawed. We hurt each other because we have been hurt, and because we're imperfect. But staying in a cycle of insecurity and hurt within the context of a friendship could lead us to some potentially dark places—it could derail us from our goals and priorities.

Motivational speaker Jim Rohn famously said that we are the average of the sum of the five people we spend the most time with. That's true. Friendships are powerful influences in our lives. Friends can greatly affect our perception of ourselves. As my friendship with Yael changed, so did my opinion of myself.

In 1999, a group of researchers conducted a study on partners—friends and romantic partners—and it showed that when our friends treat us well and believe we are who we want to be, we become more like our ideal self. Likewise, when a friend is condescending and judgmental and makes us feel like we don't measure up, it'll have a negative effect on who we become. This is called the Michelangelo effect,[1] and it's the first of five signs that a friendship is unhealthy.

1. A friend routinely makes you feel ashamed, embarrassed, or less than.

Have you ever been friends with someone who, when you leave hanging out with them, you feel a little less than? They may even make passive-aggressive comments like, "Well, I can't eat like *you* eat. You'll eat anything! You're *so* lucky to not have to diet all the time!" Or maybe it's a friend who is directly insulting. "You can never hang out. You're always working. You're always training. You're always with your family." These kinds of comments are okay if they're from friends who helpfully point out our blind spots. But the motive behind these here isn't helpful, it's indicting.

I had a friend who was vegan who I could never eat meat around because she'd make the most judgmental comments. She even broke out a pretty graphic YouTube video once when I ordered grilled chicken at lunch. But because I'm an athlete who needs a ton of protein to perform, I realized that if not eating meat was a requisite to being her friend, I needed to put that friendship on the bench. That's a mild example. I've seen other friends change their behavior drastically based on who their "team" or group of friends is. I've seen friends start to drink more alcohol based on their friend group. I've seen them begin to spend more money to keep up with the other girls in the group. I've seen them slack off at work or at school. And I've even seen some suffer mental health challenges because of their friend group—developing eating disorders and anxiety in an effort to fit in and stay in.

2. Your habits or lifestyle are negatively influenced by the friendship.

I can be pretty snarky. Not like negative snark, but I can certainly be sarcastic. But here's what I know: There's a time and a place for sarcasm. And it's not *all* the time. But if you spend too much time with people who are constantly cynical, bitter, or sarcastic, that's inevitably going to rub off on you. It's the same idea as scrolling through social media during a presidential election year. You get so grossed out and turned off by all the back-and-forth negativity that you end up feeling either anxious, angry, or exhausted. So you stay off social media.

The same advice could be given for a friend who is constantly negative. If a friend consistently complains, can't find anything encouraging to say, and who is always a Debbie Downer, there's a problem. You can't exist under those conditions without you, too, sharing in their whine-fest. Misery loves company, but don't let that company be you.

3. The relationship is codependent.

Have you ever dated a stage-five clinger? I dated this guy once who, after our second date, asked if I wanted to share locations.

Um, what? Stalk, much?

I obviously didn't agree to share locations *and* I didn't agree to a third date. But clingy or needy people don't just come in the form of romantic partners. You can have friends who will suck the life from your soul if you'll let them. These are the friends who get jealous and upset if they see a photo you posted with any other friend besides them. This is the friend who will call back-to-back-to-back if you don't answer the phone. They'll click the "?" emphasis on their last text if you don't answer them in under five minutes.

These are the friends you walk on eggshells around. And if you think about it…You can't actually *walk* on eggshells without crushing them. Trying to please these people is the same level of impossibility. You may as well try to force water out of a stone. These types of friends are tricky because, for a time, they can make us feel really good about ourselves. We're wanted. We're needed. They're always in crisis and we're always their source of solution. But this is where we have to recognize codependency for what it is—an excessive reliance on one person to meet all of our emotional needs.

4. The relationship is draining.

If there's a friend whose name you dread seeing pop up on your phone, it's important you do some introspection as to why. Do they talk about themselves for half an hour straight, then rush off the phone like *you've* been dominating the conversation? Are they always complaining or gossiping? Do they reach out to you only when they need something? Or do they seem incapable of making a decision *without* your input? If there are relationships in your life that subtract more than they add, they need to be evaluated. Maybe a conversation can adjust the boundaries. But maybe it's a friendship that you've outgrown.

5. Your friend isn't trustworthy—something doesn't add up about their motives.

This may sound like two signs in one, but really, liars are almost always narcissistic and narcissists are almost always liars.

My inner circle is the dream team—it's incredible. I couldn't ask for a better group of women to love and support me.

Like I've said, I've had some experience with narcissists and people who tried to (or did) gaslight me. You want to know something, though? *I saw it coming.* Every time! When I look back at instances where I've been hurt personally and professionally, I had a feeling about that person's lack of character long before they showed it to me. Some people call it "gut instinct" or "intuition," some even say it's the spirit of God that lives inside believers. But every time I've ignored that feeling about someone, I've paid for it in the end.

I've also had narcissists come in and out of my inner circle, but they don't stay around long. Why? Because over the years I've learned the value of being direct with the people who are closest to me. Narcissists tend to hate direct communication because it's more difficult for them to manipulate conversations or gaslight you.

"Gaslight" is a term that's become popular in recent years. Essentially, to gaslight someone is to twist words, actions, and circumstances in your favor. People who gaslight others are never at fault—ever. They can turn any situation around to be the victim. People who gaslight others are almost always narcissists with a history of tension-filled or broken relationships.

I had a friend that we'll call Michelle. Michelle and I met through mutual acquaintances and we hit it off right away. Michelle was *loud*. She didn't care what people thought of her. She was a sports fanatic like me. And she was fun. When Michelle was around, there was a flurry of activity, laughter, music, and glitter. Okay, maybe not the glitter part. But her life *did* seem to sparkle.

But I noticed something about Michelle. She talked dirt about every person in her life. We'd go to dinner with a group of friends and on the way home she'd text me, laying into one of the girls we'd just hung out with. "She's put on weight." Or, "I never thought she'd shut up!" Or, "You know she's been in trouble with the police before, right?" Just divulging secrets and gossiping like we hadn't just shared a meal together.

The first time this happened, I should have known that Michelle was not the kind of friend I needed. I had a feeling that if I stayed in the friendship, it wouldn't be long before she was telling *my* secrets. But I told myself, *Scout, you're just paranoid. You don't trust people. You've got to give this girl a chance.*

A few months into our friendship, we went to a birthday party together. I had to leave early to catch a flight, so I left in an

Uber before the party ended. I was a few minutes into my ride when I got a text from her. When I opened it, it was clear that the text was *not* intended for me.

Because it was about me.

When it comes to your own life, trust your instincts with relationships. If things aren't adding up, there's usually a reason. Whatever your intuition, your instincts, your spirit is telling you about somebody, listen to that. I have learned in my life that whenever I have followed those feelings, they've never led me wrong about a person. But whenever I've gone against them, whenever I've ignored the red flags, whenever I've tried to justify a behavior or action, I've always regretted it.

So I'm gonna find the best processes, the best coach, the best medical team, the best manager, the best agent, the best mentors, the best friends that I can. I'm going to make sure that we're all aligned on the same page. That we're all doing this for the right reasons. That we all have the same goals in mind. I want my life and my career to be purposeful and impact-driven. So I'm not putting people on my team who are not doing this for an impactful or purposeful reason.

For me, it's less about the wins and the losses and it's more about "Okay. How can we work together to do good? To create change? To fight for equity and inclusion?" Those are the things that are important to me.

Even though you're probably not hiring an actual teammate, the same principles apply. If someone isn't in your life for the right reasons, you are better off without that friendship. One of the best things that happened to me was the failure of 2018. When I looked around, there weren't many people left standing in my corner. But those people—those loyal, real OGs—those are my people. Don't look for who stands beside you in the sunshine. Look for the people standing beside you in the storm.

I think it's worth mentioning here, too, that we need to be self-aware enough to know when *we're* the friend that needs to be cut. When *we're* the shamer, the bad influence, the storm cloud, the drainer, or the user. I'll raise my hand and admit that I haven't always been the perfect friend.

I heard a pastor named Jeff Henderson give a talk once about soliciting feedback from the most important people in our lives. He told us to send a text or email to five to seven people and ask a simple question: "What's it like to be on the other side of me?"

I was surprised by some of the responses that I got. Like, *Dang, tell me how you really feel!* But it also provided an opportunity for me to grow. For me to improve. For me to become a better friend and role model to the people I care about most.

Because the very *best* way to attract the right kind of teammate is to be the teammate to others that you want to find.

CHAPTER NINE

YOUR INFLUENCE

There's this buzz phrase right now in inclusion circles: "a seat at the table." In other words, an influential voice in a conversation that leads to decision-making. For people with disabilities, we have very few seats at very few tables. We have fewer seats than minorities, and fewer seats than women. Because think about it—you can think of examples of minorities and females in positions of power. But can you think of one person with a disability?

In fact, it's difficult to get anyone to see that people with disabilities are even a marginalized group. When organizations and companies have conversations about diversity, equity, and inclusion, they're talking about hiring and promoting more women, more people of color, and more members of the LGBTQ community. Disabled people aren't even in the equation. We have no visibility because we're not thought of as being on the same level of cognitive capabilities as able-bodied people. Despite being the "nation's largest minority,"[1] people with disabilities remain invisible in leadership roles and positions of influence.

As a female from a minority with a disability, it used to be hard for me to get in the *building*, much less in the room or take a seat at the table. Over the years, especially the last few, my success on the track has garnered a few invitations to tables I have been honored to sit at. But what I've realized about many of these tables is that I'm there for show. My chair may as well be out in the parking lot. I'm there to check a box. "See, we have a minority woman with a disability at our table. We are WOKE."

Having a seat at the table is important, but if you're not valuing my seat and you're just using me as a way to check a box, you're not creating change. So while I'm still committed to finding meaningful seats at tables where I can influence change for the betterment of people with disabilities, female athletes, and minorities, I've also decided that I don't have time to wait around. If 2020 taught us anything, it taught us that nothing in this life is a guarantee and *everything* can change overnight. I don't know how long I'll have anyone's ear, so the time to act is now.

With all this in mind, I made a decision: I'm building my own table.

Looking back, I feel like a lot of the decisions and the choices I've made in my life have been part of my path toward building my own table. I haven't felt compelled to beg for somebody to have me at their table, plus I really like the idea of building a table of my own. Because if you wait for other people to accept you at their table, that's not power—that's not real influence. But you can take back your power and influence by building a new table. For me, it's about building a world that I want to live in—building a world I want to see.

Together with my team, we've started a fund called the Scout Bassett Fund. (Okay, I didn't say it was a particularly creative name. We're still working on it.) In addition to raising awareness of athletes with disabilities, telling their stories, and celebrating their pursuits, we're going to give money to disabled women who want to train to be elite athletes. That way, we are removing one less tripwire in the minefield of disabled sports. And I'm not talking about a few thousand dollars. We've had a partner give a very generous donation that will allow us to give five-figure grants to these girls who have no chance at a blue-chip sponsor because they're not able-bodied athletes. This will give these girls the financial support and resources they need to focus on their passion for sport.

Why does building my own table mean so much to me? Because there's *so much* at stake. What's at stake is the life, experience, and opportunity of every disabled girl that I mentor. And not just them, but the generation after them, and the generation after that. If I can't use my voice and my platform to improve the world for the people who come after me, I have no meaningful legacy.

Because trust me—the life, experience, and opportunity of a disabled female in America is not one I'd wish on anyone.

LIVING IN THE MARGINS

I was on a flight home to San Diego recently and when the plane landed, like clockwork everyone started standing up to deplane. I really don't understand this logic—standing up in order to wait to exit. Why not just stay seated? I've seen people stand up before the plane has come to a full stop. I guess people are antsy, but ain't no one getting off the plane until the person in front of them gets off the plane first. I'd rather enjoy a few more minutes of stillness before the madness of an airport.

But I digress.

It was my turn to exit the plane, and because I'm so short, I couldn't reach my carry-on in the overhead compartment. It had slid backward behind my seat. The lady behind me glanced down at my prosthetic and with a look of sympathy said, "Don't worry, honey. I'll get that for you."

She handed me my bag, I thanked her and hurried down the aisle before I made someone wait ten seconds longer than they expected, and lest I receive another heavy sigh and eyeroll.

I entered the terminal and was opening the Uber app on my phone when I felt a tap on my shoulder. I turned. It was the lady who helped me with my bag.

"Thank you for your service," she said. "Which branch did you serve in? My son did three tours in Afghanistan as a marine."

Now, here's where you might be thinking, *What? Why would someone make the assumption that Scout served in the military just because she has a missing leg?* But this is not an uncommon experience for me. I get asked almost every time I'm in an airport by at least one person if I lost my leg while on active duty in the military. This is true—I couldn't make this up if I tried.

And their reaction is the same every time.

"Actually," I said, "I lost my leg in a fire as an infant."

And just like that, I'm discussing the most horrific moment of my life with a complete and total stranger. A stranger whose expression morphs from misty-eyed wonder to clear disappointment.

"Oh," she said, suddenly very interested in her purse strap. She stuttered, "Well...sorry for your loss," before hurrying away.

As she retreated, I wanted to say "Well, I didn't *die*," but I managed to wrangle my tongue in time.

This is just one story of a hundred that I can tell about what it's like to be not just a person with a disability, but a female with a disability. If you look at our culture, women with disabilities are largely viewed as weak and deficient, whereas we see men with disabilities as being heroes and honorable and brave and courageous. For the most part, we associate amputees with combat. Like, if you're a dude and you're under the age of fifty with an amputation, people think, *Oh, he must be a veteran. He's a hero. He's brave. He's courageous.* And then we cheer and clap for him.

Once people learn I'm a run-of-the-mill, accident-related amputee, I suddenly become very unimportant. I'm not the only female amputee who gets questioned regarding my status as a vet. Other women I know with disabilities get it, too. And they get the same reaction. People are so disappointed. Meanwhile, they have no idea what your story is. They don't know that living in the orphanage was like being in a war. And not that I'd ever compare my experience to someone fighting for their country, but I was constantly fighting to stay alive. This is not an exaggeration. Even as a young kid I knew I was fragile. I knew I wouldn't live to see adulthood if my living conditions persisted.

The few females with disabilities that we've seen portrayed on television have, for the most part, been evil or dark characters. Take the 2020 film *The Witches* starring Anne Hathaway. In this adaptation of Roald Dahl's novel, Hathaway plays one of three witches who have deformed hands with three fingers. In Dahl's book, the witches didn't have hands with three fingers—that detail was added to make the witches come across as scarier and more sinister.

Immediately following the film, the hashtag #NotAWitch trended on Twitter. People were upset—I was one of those people. Like, why does a disability equate innate creepiness? Evil witch-ness? Lucky Fin Project, a nonprofit project that raises awareness for those of us with limb differences, released a film featuring adults and children with limb differences talking about their disabilities in light of *The Witches*. The film tanked, and Hathaway—to her credit—issued an apology on her Instagram:

> I particularly want to say I'm sorry to kids with limb differences: now that I know better I promise I'll do better. And I owe a special apology to everyone who loves you as fiercely as I love my own kids: I'm sorry I let your family down...[2]

Anne, I forgive you. But it's difficult to forget the thought process behind the hand and finger revision.

But that's how we portray women with disabilities. There's something wrong with us. There has never been a queen or princess or character embodying goodness played by a female with a disability. Ever. In fact, our disability often becomes evil personified. It's like we're evil, we're deficient, we're weak. After a lifetime of messages that I'm less than—even in how I *became* disabled—it would be easy to buy into the lie that I have no influence. It would be logical to infer that, based on how society treats us, girls and women who don't meet the "status quo" have no voice. That our potential to enact meaningful change is nonexistent.

Maybe that's a message you've received throughout your life, too. Maybe you've been convinced that, because you aren't "normal" enough, you can't or shouldn't speak up for yourself or for others.

I've fought against this categorization my entire career. If you listen to sports commentators during the Paralympics, you'll hear them refer to our disability as something we've had to "overcome" in order to be successful. As a result Paralympians are praised as "superheroes."[3] But it's as if we can never just be an athlete. We can never just be strong or disciplined or good at our sport. There's always a superlative attached to our achievement, and underneath the praise is something more like "She's doing well...for someone with one leg." There is a name for this type of representation—supercrip[4]—and it's prevalent in the sports world and culture.

Look, I get it. It's not easy to talk about Paralympic athletes without mentioning our disability. But maybe some of us don't attach the same amount of shame or the same amount of disappointment to not being able-bodied. I don't know many able-bodied athletes who would put themselves through the absolute torture of training with a prosthetic. Mine is an extension of who I am—but it's not *who* I am. While I'm proud to represent the disabled athlete community, my identity as an athlete who works her ass off should be at the forefront of how I'm represented.

We've already talked about how women are often judged based on their physical appearance, and how prevalent it is, as well as imbalanced. And I think that plays a role in the way women with disabilities are represented in society. So if you're a woman and you have a physical imperfection, the world can't possibly view you as worthy or desirable. And you certainly can't be "hot."

Every now and then I'll get guys sliding into my DMs and they say the most ridiculous things. A lot of my girlfriends with disabilities get this, too. More often than not, here's how the message generally goes:

Oh my goodness, you're so beautiful. You're so pretty. You're stunning—you're gorgeous...for someone with a disability.

It's even worse when they say it in person. Because I know what they're implying, and they won't say it exactly like they would in a message, but it's usually something along the lines of, "Oh, you're even more beautiful in person—you're prettier than I expected."

I probably don't handle those moments well. I'm sure I roll my eyes. It's like, *Yeah. Okay. I know what you're implying here. I understand all the nuances of what you're trying to say.*

My point in telling you this is that this is *not* the case for men with disabilities. They never get told, "Hey, you're hot for a guy with a disability."

San Diego has this great community of men who are injured vets, and I'm friends with a lot of those guys. I also have other male friends who have limb differences who aren't veterans. I've asked them, "Hey, does this happen to you?"

Nope. Never.

But the idea is that a woman can't be both disabled and attractive. And, hey, to a certain degree, I get it. We look in the mirror every day and we see the things we can't change about ourselves. We know we're not the beauty "ideal." What we don't need is other people pointing this out to us. It's like you spend your whole life grappling with this aspect of yourself that is beyond your control, you know you're not ever going to measure up by society's standard of beauty, and day after day people lean into that wound with assumptions.

In terms of exclusion, the beauty and the fashion industry are the worst. And it makes sense, right? Because as a society, we see a person's beauty and value based on their physical appearance. And when it comes to having a disability, there's something visually that throws people off. That makes people uncomfortable. We see someone in a wheelchair and they seem to be struggling, or we see someone with a prosthetic and they seem to be hobbling or not walking too well. It's just something that people don't like to see—like domestic abuse or homelessness. You want to turn your head and look a different direction.

To a degree, I understand this. Our eyes aren't trained to process physical disabilities because there are few to no examples in mainstream media to give them context.

It's funny, because every now and then I'll mess with people when I'm out in public. Like, if I'm wearing something that exposes my prosthetic and I'm walking somewhere, people will pass me and then they'll do a double take. Like, *Did I just see what I think I saw?* So when someone walks by, I'll wait for a couple of seconds and then I'll turn around and 99 percent of the time I'll catch them staring at me, trying to make sense of my missing leg.

I haven't always felt as comfortable as I do now with my body. And I still have days where the stares, the comments, and the pervasive exclusiveness of society gets to me. But I can tell you this—I didn't start feeling confident about who I am and how I was created until I started using my voice, my influence, to speak up for myself and others.

INVITING PEOPLE TO THE TABLE

One cause that I'm magnetically drawn to use my influence for is female representation at the Paralympics. The number of opportunities for female Paralympic athletes is disgracefully lower than those for men. We get the crap training times and tracks, fewer scholarship dollars, and only 4 percent of media coverage.[5] Four.

But the marginalization doesn't end there. Especially when you compare Olympic athletes to Paralympic athletes. Historically, Olympic athletes have won significantly more prize dollars than Paralympic athletes. Now, who do you think has to train and work harder? An able-bodied athlete or an athlete who might have gotten a new running prosthetic months before the competition, which is the equivalent of learning how to compete on a brand-new leg?

The Tokyo Games were the first for which Paralympic and Olympic athletes were paid the same. And the Games were also the first during which the Paralympics were given a decent amount of mainstream media coverage. These are two giant leaps toward equity. But we're still not there. We're not even very close.

In my sport alone—track and field—we have seventeen fewer medal events than the men. And that's already the decided program for the 2024 Games in Paris. Seventeen events multiplied by three (gold, silver, bronze) is fifty-one fewer opportunities.

It's not just the medals. Fewer events also means that all these women who could have competed aren't going to be able to even go to the Games—like my experience in Tokyo in 2021. Another fifty-one times a woman is denied the opportunity to expand her platform and become more visible. Fifty-one missed chances to get on the podium, to make money, and to get the attention of sponsors. Fifty-one fewer opportunities to support themselves and their families.

If you zoom out and take a look at the Paralympic sports broadly—not just track and field—women make up only about 38 percent of the competitors compared to the nearly fifty-fifty even split between able-bodied men and women in the Olympics. Female Paralympic athletes also competed in thirty-eight fewer events than Paralympic men.[6] Now we're looking at 114 fewer opportunities and 114 more missed chances. And if you want to zoom out one last time, the National Federation of State High School Associations reports that boys get 1.13 *million* more sport opportunities than girls do.[7] If *that* number doesn't rattle you, I need you to check yourself for a pulse.

The argument is very chicken-or-the-egg. We're told that we don't have as many events because the participation numbers are not there for women in those events. Okay, but are the participation numbers not there because you don't even offer the events in the first place? How is a young girl supposed to train for an event that currently isn't even offered at the Paralympics? What is her motivating factor? Until those events are created and opened up for women, it's highly unlikely that girls will train for them. Which leaves us pretty stuck from where I'm sitting.

A young girl I am mentoring right now is going to go to a Pac-12 school—so a Division I college—and she's planning to play wheelchair tennis as part of their club wheelchair tennis team. But the most they have offered her in scholarship money won't even come close to covering tuition.

Since she's going to have to pay out-of-state tuition, she might as well be paying her own way entirely. Meanwhile, she will likely represent our country at the next Paralympic Games. The incongruency between those two facts astounds me. America thinks you're good enough to represent them on sport's biggest stage, but America isn't willing to invest in your athleticism or your education to help you get there or win there. You can win a medal for your country, but because you aren't able-bodied, you need to foot the bill for the training, equipment, coaching, and travel to get there.

To me it's just absolutely bizarre. Why should she be denied the opportunity to earn a full athletic scholarship just like her able-bodied counterparts? But right now, our society doesn't notice this disparity. The accepted view is that you can earn a real scholarship only if you are able to compete or run or swim or jump at an able-bodied standard. What we know about people with disabilities is that that standard cannot be the same. Take me, for example. I'm missing my leg from above the knee down. I'm never going to be able to run an able-bodied time. I mean, I can't even build out my quad muscles on that side because I don't have a knee socket!

In the Olympic community, college is an incredible feeder program for Olympic sports. But at the Paralympic level, there is no feeder program. And there are very few opportunities for these athletes to continue to train and compete throughout their college years because the money and resources aren't available. Right now, there's really not a development program for disabled athletes that goes beyond high school.

Moving forward, there has got to be a system put in place where you can still have a disability and compete collegiately and it's not measured by the same criteria as we measure able-bodied performances and results. For me, that's where I think building my own table can really make a difference. I think there's a huge opportunity that's missed here because these athletes are incredible.

We continue to be limited, and I'm convinced it's due largely in part to a lack of representation at the decision-making level. We don't have a seat at the table. While the International Olympic Committee (IOC) has made efforts to include women—disabled women, too—at the leadership level, I feel there's still so much work to be done.

In 2020, Women in Sports released its seventh volume of synthesized research[8] on women in the Olympic and Paralympic movement. The IOC set a goal for female membership of 30 percent, and in 2020, 36.3 percent of its members were female. I'm not going to clap my hands for a goal of one in three because that's still not equitable, but I'll give them a nod for trying to decrease the gap. Only four women (26.7 percent) sit on the IOC executive board, and there's never been a female IOC president. Out of the 205 National Olympic Committees, only 9.8 percent have female presidents, and a mind-blowing 77.6 percent have all-male leadership teams.

As for the International Paralympic Committee (IPC), only four out of fourteen governing positions are held by women. Both the IPC president and vice president are men and, like the IOC, there has never been a female IPC president. Out of 181 National Paralympic Committees, men make up 80.5 percent of presidents and 67.6 percent of all main contacts.

That's a lot of data coming at you fast, but all you need to really know is this: Good intentions—like threshold goals for female representation—can move the needle, but if the expectation isn't an even fifty-fifty split, what are we even doing?

This "take what you can get" mindset is another reason I decided to invite female Paralympic hopefuls to my table. They don't have a voice. They don't have a champion. They don't have anyone sitting in their corner and fighting for them. In an industry where one in three is supposed to shut us up and make us "thankful," they're set up to struggle and set up to fail.

These injustices—and many more that I could talk about—keep me up at night. They stir a thirst inside me for something better. Despite being marginalized, despite being made to feel like an other, I know I can't stay silent. What influence I do have, I have to leverage for good. The same is true for you. You may feel like a nobody. You may feel that even if you did try to use your influence to help others, no one would listen or it wouldn't matter. First, I don't believe that's true. For the person or people you are trying to help, your support and efforts on their behalf could be just what they need to keep moving forward. And second, it's not *just* about the outcomes.

I've been speaking out on behalf of female Paralympians for a while now, and there hasn't been much measurable change. But using my influence in this way has not only been good for my soul, but it's given others like me permission to join in and raise their voices as well. When we use our influence for good, even though we may not be able to see an instant difference in our cause, momentum and synergy are built. You may be building the foundation for the movement you're using your influence to fight for.

The main idea behind the Scout Bassett Fund is to allow these young women to train their way into Paralympic contention. But it's also a way to give these young women a megaphone—to give them a chance to build their own platforms so that they can join their voices with mine to fight for equality and to fight for better representation of disabled females on and off the track.

My question for you is simple: What tables do you sit at that you could invite others to? If that answer is none, are you willing to build your own table? I'm not saying you have to start a foundation or a fund. Building your own table could look a number of different ways based on the building supplies you have access to.

Are you a manager at a store who could hire or promote disabled or immigrant workers?

Do you have social influence or clout you could leverage to bring awareness to an underserved demographic?

Could you lend your voice to share the narratives of the oppressed and marginalized?

Who are you reaching back for to pull up with you? Whose future are you trying to remove limits from? I believe we're never more powerful or influential than when we're giving away our power and influence to those a few steps behind us. Who are you empowering, championing, and advocating for? Who are you inviting to sit at your table?

I grew up feeling like I didn't have many options. In my orphanage days, I could hardly go to the bathroom without someone helping me, much less do something important, helpful, or meaningful. I felt powerless. And the consistent message I've received since coming to this country has largely been shaming. In our society I'm either left out completely, vilified, or portrayed as incapable.

But at some point, I decided to push back. To resist the mindset that "different" means "weak." I have something to offer this world. You do, too. We all have a voice—influence. We all have the ability to stand up for someone who is a few steps or years behind us. Whether it be by encouraging them personally or including and praising them publicly.

Yes, now I have choices. Now I have a voice. But I haven't always. It wasn't until I started using my voice for others that my confidence grew. With my confidence, my influence grew, too.

It doesn't matter where you've come from, what you look like, or what your story has been so far.

Being powerful and influential isn't about being the loudest. Being powerful and influential is about using your voice for those without one.

CHAPTER TEN

BEING A CHAMPION

There's really no greater satisfaction than in doing something that people didn't think you could do. The word "champion" is typically associated with the person standing on the center of the podium during a medal ceremony. My whole life, all I wanted was to be that person—the one receiving the gold. I've stood there, leaning over as the medal was placed over my head while my country's national anthem played. I can tell you that in those moments, you're not thinking about the people who held you back. You're thinking about the road you traveled to get where you're standing right then.

Becoming a champion requires every bit of you. And there are *plenty* of lessons to learn on the road to gold. But one of the most valuable lessons I learned came from my previous coach, former US Olympic hurdler Tonie Campbell. He'd say, "A real champion doesn't just develop their skills when they're on the track. A real champion is a champion on *and off* the track."

Becoming a champion isn't parttime work. If you spend five hours a day training and working on the qualities of becoming a champion on the track—the strength, the technique, the endurance, the physical capacity—you've got to devote just as much time to the qualities of being a champion off the track, the inner qualities. You've got to hone your perseverance, your resilience, your fortitude, your mental health. You've got to be a champion on the inside before you can ever become a champion on the outside.

BUILDING YOUR INNER CHAMP

I didn't come from a particularly athletic family. My parents didn't play sports, and they weren't really into them as spectators, either. None of my siblings played sports. And because I grew up in the orphanage in Nanjing, I didn't even know sports existed until I came to the United States.

You'll hear a lot of interviews with professional athletes who knew they wanted to compete because of someone famous they saw play on TV. Because they watched Kobe play for the Lakers, or Serena and Venus at Wimbledon, or Shaun White on the slopes. They saw what was possible at the highest level and they set their sights on achieving the same amount of success. Not me. I fell in love with sports because it brought me two things I desperately craved: (1) joy and (2) connection.

I remember the first time I saw a group of kids playing soccer at school. At the time, I could hardly speak a word of English. I felt trapped in my own mind and I wasn't doing well academically. We went outside for recess and a group of kids started to kick around a black and white ball. Everybody on the field was smiling and laughing. I might not have been able to speak the language, but I could interpret facial expressions. They were having *fun*. I had no idea what I was looking at, but I knew I wanted to try it. I wanted to be a part of something—I wanted to feel *whole*.

As we've already discussed, I would go on to spend the better part of the next decade on the sidelines. I was always welcome to come to practice, welcome to do the drills, welcome to be on the team, but I was certainly not welcome to play. It sort of felt like the always-a-bridesmaid cliché of sports. But when Stan fitted me with my running prosthetic and encouraged me to enter my first race, I had a monster meltdown, as I mentioned. We're talking *epic* proportions. Snot, tears, all of it. I didn't want to do it. But that memory of seeing the smiles and hearing that laughter found its way to the forefront of my thoughts.

This could be my chance... I dared to dream. I always look back at this decision to run, this decision to believe something more could be possible for me as the first step I took toward my inner champion.

1. Dare to dream.

Running became my freedom. It became my hope—my purpose. Running gave me a place to belong. Running was the one sport where I couldn't get benched. Running was who I became.

I don't know if you're a dreamer or not. Maybe you used to be one, but the harsh reality of life has you jaded or cynical. Maybe you chased your dreams for a while, but came up short. So you've settled for the status quo and struggle with feelings of unfulfillment. Or maybe you feel like your "time" has passed. As an athlete approaching my mid-thirties, I feel you. But one quality of an inner champion that serves as a catalyst for all the others is the ability to dream—the ability to believe that the unlikely is possible for you.

I can't do this work for you. And I can't even really tell you how to do it for yourself. I would encourage you to begin journaling about your dreams or to take a friend to coffee and exchange the dreams you have for your lives. Verbalizing what you dream for yourself helps manifest the energy and positivity that are required for making those dreams come true.

I didn't start out as a sprinter. It was the opposite, actually. I started out with distance running and competitive triathlons through the Challenged Athletes Foundation. I continued running and training, not sure what the end goal was outside of the feeling running gave me. This was all before there were sports prosthetics—before I really even knew of amputees doing athletics, and so growing up running was very experimental, which brought its own set of challenges.

I didn't know about Paralympics growing up, but I did know I had to get out of my hometown. My parents weren't pushy people. They didn't encourage me to play sports or to go to college, but there was a fire inside of me that could not be put out. I was leaving. And if it were up to me, I'd never be coming back.

Fast-forward to UCLA. I had earned a full merit scholarship to go there. I had promised my classmates and teacher that that's what I was going to do, and no one believed me. One word about your dreams: Don't share them with people who don't respect you. They'll only try to hold you back to make themselves feel better about not having any dreams of their own.

You can probably tell from the number of stories I've shared from my college experience that it was an incredible chapter of my life. I'm still so proud to be a Bruin! But one of the things that happened when I was at school is that in my sophomore year, I got approached by Cathy Sellers, who was the director of Paralympic Track and Field for Team USA.

"I hear you're a runner," Cathy said. "Have you thought of the Paralympics?"

That was maybe the second most magical moment of life—second to getting my running blade and competing in that first race. As a girl who always wanted to be an elite-level athlete but was never seen that way? I didn't even have to think about it. I think my exact words were, "Sign me up." Later I'd find out that they were trying to recruit more disabled female athletes because our numbers at the Paralympics were just so low.

At the time, I was coming from a triathlon and endurance running background, so they knew I could run. But I had never done track before. We didn't even have a track program at my high school. But the opportunity to compete at the Paralympics among the very best athletes in the world was very attractive to me.

"Where do I start?" I asked.

Cathy told me to contact one of the track-and-field coaches at UCLA to see if I could join or do some workouts with the team or even separately. She told me to ask if one of the coaches might be able to work with me knowing that I was now training to go to the 2012 Paralympics in London.

The University of California, Los Angeles had a stellar track program. So I went to one of the coaches and I asked her if I could train with the team. I made it clear that I was obviously not asking for the same services or benefits that team members enjoyed. That would have been presumptuous. I wasn't competing for the school and I wasn't there on an NCAA scholarship. I recognized all those facts. But what I *was* looking for was a chance. An opportunity. A place to run.

"I'm sorry," the coach said. "But no."

She explained that there were legal liabilities and that she wouldn't even know where to start in training a disabled athlete.

I did understand, but it was still very frustrating. I sat at a cross-roads after that conversation. Do I give up? Do I call Cathy and tell her, "Thanks, but no thanks"? I was at a crossroads. Another pivotal circumstance in my journey where my life could have gone a totally different direction. I consulted my inner champion: *What do we do next?* I decided to bet on myself.

2. Bet on you.

Another quality of inner champions is valuing themselves enough to be self-reliant. Someone who isn't deterred by momentary set-backs. Someone who doesn't make excuses, but creates results. People who bet on themselves don't hitch their goals or ambitions onto anyone else's horse but themselves. When obstacles arise, they simply figure it out for themselves—they take matters and outcomes into their own hands.

So that's what I did. I started training on my own, having very little knowledge of what it takes to become a Paralympic sprinter.

I woke up super early in the mornings before UCLA's team was on the track and I just started running. When I think back to those dark-thirty training sessions, I almost want to laugh at my methods. I'd line up, sprint. Line up, sprint. And line up and sprint again. I found some YouTube videos at some point on different exercises and modalities I could use to improve my performance, but for the most part, I was out there winging it.

As an aside, the UCLA assistant coach I spoke with has since reached out to me and apologized. "I knew nothing about the Paralympics," she said. "And I thought you were just a student wanting to run and work out with my team. And our practices were closed to all other students."

It's all right, Coach. I managed just fine.

The program that I'm doing now was created by my former coach. She was the head women's track coach at a West Coast college, and has a model that I think is translatable for colleges everywhere to allow Paralympic hopefuls to train and work out. I know so many schools or coaches are intimidated by the idea of reinventing the wheel. They think, *Oh we've got to create a whole program for athletes with disabilities,* and my reply is that it's not as difficult as you might think.

The way you train an able-bodied athlete is similar to the way you train a disabled athlete. The workouts aren't that different because the technique that's required for an able-bodied sprinter to be great is very similar to what I need to do to be great. Obviously, there are going to be modifications and things that will need to change in order for me to be able to do some of the drills and some of the workouts, but it's really not all that different or difficult.

I reject the idea that integration isn't possible. It's not unrealistic to have one or two athletes with disabilities as part of your able-bodied program. Again, we just need to have leaders, coaches, and people in positions of authority who have the willingness and the open-minded approach of working with somebody with a disability.

I've obviously been so lucky to train with top coaches, but I know many disabled athletes who haven't been afforded the same opportunity.

So I bet on myself, training alone the best way I knew how. I showed up for the 2012 London trials feeling doubtful but excited. I'd been in the sport for two years but was anxious to see how the standings shook out. As you already know, the only thing shaking after that race was your girl. I wasn't even *close* to making the Paralympic team. If last place had a subcategory, like, *last* last? That's what place I came in. As far as I had come, I still had so much work to do.

3. Be willing to put in the work.

That brings us to the third quality of an inner champ—be willing to put in the work.

Have you ever met someone who just expects people to do things for them? (Are you that person?) Someone who never takes responsibility for anything and is always pointing the finger at someone or something else as their reason for failure?

Why did you fail math? "My teacher sucked. He didn't know how to teach."

Why didn't you turn in the report on time? "My team really dropped the ball. They were supposed to help me."

Why is your house a wreck? "I work all day. I have no energy when I get home."

Why did your relationship fail? "He pushed me to cheat."

Why did you never go back to school? "It was too hard to balance everything with school in the equation."

Why haven't you gone to the gym? "All those skinny girls walk around in their skimpy workout clothes—I think it's disgusting."

Why haven't you started that business yet? "The process is too complicated. I can't figure it out by myself."

These types of people just make me want to cuss. Because if an orphan girl with one leg from China can win a national title at age thirty-three...I have a hard time hearing you.

I remember when I was in elementary and middle school, my education wasn't all that important to me. We didn't go to school at the orphanage, so when I was dropped into kindergarten when I came to America, I had no context for academics. By the time I got to middle school, I realized something: If I'm ever going to get out of this town, I'm going to have to get a full ride to college. So I decided to buckle down. Instead of reading arbitrary biographies and memorizing spelling bee lists, I started to study the actual curriculum. I started engaging in class discussions, preparing for tests, and giving maximum effort on every assignment.

I went from making average grades to graduating with a 4.8 GPA and, as you know, getting a scholarship to attend UCLA.

Let me tell you something I've realized: There's always going to be an excuse to *not* put in the work. To not stretch yourself and to not push yourself. And some of those excuses are valid. You are probably busy—everyone is. You are probably overwhelmed—everyone is. You probably aren't sure exactly what to do—no one really is. As humans, we avoid discomfort like it may kill us. (Spoiler alert: It won't!) But when we fail to reach our goals, I think more often than not, the most honest reason is, "I didn't put in the work."

After the London trials it would have been easy to throw up my hands and say, "Well, I tried!" But that's not what I did. I went back to work. When you're talking about training for the Olympics or Paralympics, it's not like training for any other sport. There are *four years* between events. Four. Years. That's one heck of a commitment. But a year later, I was able to compete in the US National Championships, where I went from worst to first, winning the gold in the 100-meter sprint. How did I get there?

It was time to make some sacrifices. That's the next quality of the inner champion.

4. Be willing to sacrifice for what you want.
I graduated from UCLA and went to work for a prosthetics

company in Orange County. The job wasn't *my* dream. It might have been what others expected from me, but it wasn't what I expected from myself. It was time for me to stop straddling both worlds, trying to make everyone happy—everyone besides me. I knew I had to make a difficult choice: continue working for the medical device company and give up training, or risk it all and quit my job to become a full-time professional athlete.

You know which I chose.

In 2015 I quit living someone else's version of my life and started to live my own. In hindsight, this sounds sort of romantic. It sounds brave and daring and like an adventure. But honestly, in many ways, it was hell.

I had saved up a little money before I left my job. I budgeted twenty-five dollars per week for food, most of which consisted of various flavors of ramen noodles. I slept most nights in my 1992 Toyota Corolla—which was maybe the first time I was thankful to be so small. Other nights, I couch surfed or slept in the spare rooms of friends and family who hadn't yet tired of giving me a hand up. I've already told you how everybody thought I was crazy. There were times I feared they may be right.

There were groups like the Women's Sports Foundation and the Challenged Athletes Foundation that offered me grants during that time to keep me going. But $1,500 here and $2,000 there was not a living. It wasn't going to get me out of my car. That's why the Scout Bassett Fund *has* to offer larger payouts. We can't have athletes sleeping in their cars and expect them to be at their best in competition. And we *desperately* need more female Paralympic contenders.

Finally, after five months of being homeless and training all day, every day, I was offered sponsorships from a few different companies that allowed me to get a place of my own and add a little variety to my diet instead of, "Hm, should I have the chili flavored ramen or the beef flavored ramen for dinner tonight?"

For *years* later, I kept in my back seat the sleeping bag and pillow I used when I slept in my car. I even transferred them to my new car when I was able to afford one. I wanted them around as a reminder that I no longer need them. They were as symbolic to me as my burn scars. They reminded me that I've endured a lot to stand where I stand.

One day my former coach Tonie got in my car and glanced at the back seat. He gave me a look that said, *Really, Scout? Really?*

I knew what was coming next.

"Scout," he said. "It's time."

"But the reason I—"

"Scout," he spoke over my protests. "It is time."

He was right.

When I got home from training that night, I took the sleeping bag and the pillow inside. I tucked them neatly inside a closet and I still have them to this day. Relics of sacrifices made and ground gained.

The last quality of an inner champion that we'll talk about is the most important.

5. *Never give up. Ever.*

The difference between the loss at the London trials and the loss at the Tokyo trials was the difference between an amateur comic bombing a set at a coffeehouse open mic and Kevin Hart bombing a Netflix special. In 2012, I was green, mostly unnoticed, and no one expected a whole lot from me. But by 2021, I had a decade invested in the sport, and in many of those years had experienced a good bit of success on and off the track.

In 2012, I went behind the grandstand in Indianapolis and had myself a cry and then got right back to work. But in 2021, I experienced crippling grief. I experienced self-doubt, career crisis, and immeasurable anxiety. Tokyo was a disaster. Tokyo was an implosion. If it was time for me to give up, I wanted to do so gracefully.

I took a month off training and I traveled the world. I traveled around different cities in Spain. I stood in pristine water the color of a turquoise stone. I walked through caves that led to hidden beaches. I ate good food on cobblestoned streets. I drank wine with friends and I stayed up late. I rewarded the hard work I'd put into the grind of sport. And then I asked God, *Is it my time, Father? Is this the point in my career that I hang it up?*

But the more I thought about it and prayed about it, I wanted to give my body one last, fair shot to compete. I didn't want to overstay my Paralympic welcome, but I also didn't want to end on a race that had occurred within such close proximity to a significant injury.

When I announced I was going to continue training for Paris 2024, the critics came out like pigs to slop. They said I was washed up. Too old. A has-been. They said I'd peaked. Like we've talked about, I didn't let their words and judgments go any further than to add a little more fuel to the spark of my renewed determination. In June 2022, I brought home a gold medal—the National Championship in the 100 meters.

When I look back at my life, I see this quality in many of my decisions and choices. For better or for worse, Scout Bassett is a girl who just doesn't give up. My relentlessness has certainly bitten me in the butt a time or two and bugged the hell out of my coaches, friends, and family. But I'm proud of what I've accomplished through my decision to never ever give up. That's not to say I won't retire from track and field one day, but when I do, it won't be because I don't believe in myself anymore.

A COMMITMENT

As our time together in this book draws to a close, I want to ask you for a favor—for a promise. A commitment. And it's this:

Don't give up on yourself.

That might be a big ask, depending on where you are in your journey in life. Because this much I know is certain—if you've been on this planet for longer than three minutes, you've experienced some type of trauma, wounding, or deep disappointment.

I don't know, you could be right in the middle of your Tokyo trials implosion right now.

I ask that you'd dig into *your* inner champion. That you'd decide today that no matter how much it hurts, how hard you have to work, how many times you have to get back up, you won't give up on yourself. That you'll do the work to get healthy, to get healed, and to keep moving forward.

I have a friend named Jess who is a mother to two young boys who has just been diagnosed with cancer for the *eighth time*. She went in for her six-month scan a few weeks ago and afterward I got a text from her.

"Cancer's back," she said. "But hey, isn't eight a lucky number to the Chinese?" Only Jess could joke both about race and cancer at the same time.

She started her *eighth* round of treatment this week. I talked to her on the phone and she was actually upbeat. "They got new chemo chairs," she said. "The other ones smelled like burned plastic, so at least there's that."

She's positive. She's hopeful. And she's fighting. She's not giving up. When I think about stories like Jess's, I'm reminded of how trivial so much of what I worry about is. I'm reminded that there's so much more to life than the next race, the next promotion, the next social event, the next whatever, because I get to have a next *tomorrow*. I'm also reminded that *Jess* is the embodiment of a true champion. Because the stakes are high and the odds aren't great, but she's choosing to stay the course.

Okay, I lied. I need to ask you for *two* favors—two commitments. The second one is similar to the first, but for some of us, it's going to be a little bit more of a challenge.

Don't give up on each other.

These are dark times in America right now, aren't they? Thank God I love to watch sports and not the news, because I think I'd sleep better after watching a horror movie. It feels very much like we've all given up on each other. We're dying to be right. We'd way rather win an argument than win a heart. When it comes to bridges? We're not building them. We're lighting matches and watching bridges burn one after another after another.

But if we want to rise out of the ashes of a pandemic, social unrest, and economic crisis, we need each other. Start small if you have to. Bank that social media post. Sleep on the Instagram comment. Bite your tongue at the water cooler. Do your part to be a safe space for others. Now, I'm not saying you can't voice your opinion, but I am saying that we'll never heal as a country if we remain divided—we'll never heal if we give up on each other.

Besides, there are more important wars to wage. Instead of fighting to be right, fight for a person, instead.

The word "champion" has another meaning. It also means a person who fights for a cause with or for someone else. Someone like disabled female athletes. Marginalized minorities. Single parents. Foster kids. Addicts. The homeless. *These* champions of others are the ones remembered decades later, long after their days of competing are over. These types of champions are the ones who really deserve gold medals. These types of champions are the ones worth aspiring to, because the ripple effect of their work and efforts will be felt by generations to come.

I have won and I have lost, I have overcome and I have back-pedaled, but I've learned that the only guaranteed way to overcome odds and build a limitless future is to make your life a lot less about yourself and a lot more about others.

I've learned it's what you do for the people who can't do for themselves that truly makes you great—that makes you a champion.

EPILOGUE

I would be remiss to close out this book without acknowledging my source of wisdom throughout all the lessons we've talked about together. And that's God.

Talking about God makes some people uncomfortable. I understand that. I never want to come across as a "Bible-thumper," or like I'm preaching or condescending toward anyone. But the truth is, nothing that I've talked about in this book would have been possible without the hand of God on my life. In fact, I believe with every fiber of my being that without God, I would have been dead in the streets on Nanjing before I reached the age of eleven.

I wanted to share a verse with you that has been a comfort to me throughout my career—especially in those dark moments when I felt like everything was falling apart all around me and I had nowhere to go and no one to turn to: "Don't panic. I'm with you. There's no need to fear for I'm your God. I'll give you strength. I'll help you. I'll hold you steady, keep a firm grip on you" (Isaiah 41:10 MSG).

God is always with us. Always. He's our anchor in the storm. He's the hope we can cling to. He's a promise keeper and dream maker. He's long-suffering and good. And regardless of who you are, what you're about, or what you've done, He's endlessly forgiving, accepting, and loving.

If you don't have a relationship with God, I'd invite you to download the Bible App and start reading somewhere in the New Testament. Our world has done a lot of damage to God's name by twisting and turning His words to support their own beliefs and opinions. That's tragic. But if you can approach the idea of God with an open mind and open heart, you can decide for yourself what's real and true.

Of all the lessons I've learned, the ones in this book and the ones I'm still not ready to talk about, the most important lesson of my life has been to lean into God, to put my trust in Him, to do the hard work, and to let go of what happens next. He's faithful to give us strength, to hold us steady, and to keep us in His firm grip.

The reward for following God is the best unlimited future—one spent with Him for eternity in heaven.

ACKNOWLEDGMENTS

To the friends, family, colleagues, and organizations who have truly made me feel like a lucky girl, thank you. Thank you for encouraging me. For loving me. For believing even when the odds were against me. Without you this book would not exist. You have filled my life with hope, with joy, but more importantly, you have filled my life with truth.

Thank you to:

- Tonie Campbell, OLY
- Caty Zick
- Ian Cropp
- Lori Roth
- Marissa Papaconstantinou, PLY

To my family and my friends who have become family. You are my people—you are my tribe!

To Stan Patterson and my Prosthetic and Orthotic Associates family, you've made all things possible, and your love has changed my life.

My soul sister Denise Castelli, you are everything to me. Thank you for getting every "amputee prob," listening to every silly story, and walking every step of this journey together with me. When I had nothing, you cheered, supported, and loved the most. I am forever grateful; I love you forever.

To my teammates, coaches, sponsors, and partners, thank you for making this dream possible.

Immense gratitude to the Challenged Athletes Foundation for helping me get started as an athlete, and for inspiring my mission to build a more inclusive and accessible world. Being a CAF ambassador has been one of the greatest honors and privileges of my life.

To the Fedd Agency and all the hardworking staff who helped make this book possible, thank you for believing in me and my story.

To my amazing agent Lindsay Kagawa Colas and talent manager Lindsey Fitzgerald, thank you for moving mountains and teaching me to be bold and brave with my life. All that I am and all that I will ever be is due to your love and belief.

Holly Crawshaw, the fun we had putting this book together became the start of something beautiful. Thank you for pushing me to be vulnerable and courageous in this process. I'm so thankful for you! Go Braves!

To my mentees and all the young girls and women I've crossed paths with, thank you for being my inspiration and motivation. I've loved watching you shine and become incredible humans. Keep going, keep believing, keep working. Your dreams are valid!

My sunshine and my anchor, my sister Palmer Bassett Rodriguez, I love you beyond this lifetime.

To all whom I may have not named specifically, know that I haven't forgotten about you. Thank you for being part of so many special moments and continually covering me in prayer, kindness, and love.

And most of all to God, I thank you for all that you've brought me through.

NOTES

CHAPTER 1:

1. Madeline Coleman, "Dansby Swanson Becomes Hometown Hero As He Helps Childhood Team Win World Series," *Sports Illustrated*, November 2, 2021, https://www.si.com/mlb/2021/11/03/world-series-dansby-swanson-becomes-hometown-hero-as-braves-win-the-title.

2. Tim Ott, "Bethany Hamilton Biography," Biography.com, June 12, 2015, https://www.biography.com/athlete/bethany-hamilton.

3. "Bethany's Story," BethanyHamilton.com, accessed March 29, 2022, https://bethanyhamilton.com/biography.

4. "Young Surfer Tells Tale of Shark Attach," ABCNEWS.com, November 21, 2005, https://abcnews.go.com/2020/story?id=124360.

5. Chloe Hart, "Shark Attack Survivor Bethany Hamilton to Return to Qualify for the World Surf League," ABC.net, March 9, 2020, https://www.abc.net.au/news/2020-03-09/shark-attack-survivor-bethany-hamilton-rejoin-world-surf-league/12039266.

6. "NCAA External Gender Equity Review," Kaplan Hecker & Fink, August 2, 2021, https://ncaagenderequityreview.com/.

7. "Women's U.S. Soccer Team Settles Gender Discrimination Suit for $24 Million," *Morning Edition*, February 22, 2022, https://www.npr.org/2022/02/22/1082297455/womens-u-s-soccer-team-settle-gender-discrimination-suit-for-24-million.

CHAPTER 2:

1. Abraham Maslow, *Toward a Psychology of Being* (New York: Van Nostrand, 1968), 380.

2. Stanley Schacter, *The Psychology of Affiliation: Experimental Studies of the Sources of Gregariousness* (Stanford, CA: Stanford University Press, 1959), 703–719.

3. Steve Harvey, "You've Got to Follow That Dream," YouTube, January 2019, https://www.youtube.com/watch?v=BXlAm00zIOs.

CHAPTER 3:

1. David Robson, *The Expectation Effect* (New York: Henry Holt, 2022), 78.

2. "Disability Impacts All of Us," Centers for Disease Control and Prevention, October 28, 2022, https://www.cdc.gov/ncbddd/disabilityandhealth/infographic-disability-impacts-all.html

3. "See Jane 2019: An Analysis of Representations in Film and Television," Geena Davis Institute on Gender in Media, 2019, https://seejane.org/research-informs-empowers/see-jane-2019/.

4. Elaine Welteroth, *More Than Enough* (New York: Viking, 2019), 62.

CHAPTER 4:

1. Richard Weissbound et al., "Loneliness in America: How the Pandemic Has Deepened an Epidemic of Loneliness and What We Can Do About It," Making Caring Common, Harvard Graduate School of Education, February 2021, https://mcc.gse.harvard.edu/reports/loneliness-in-america.

2. "Loneliness and Social Isolation Linked to Serious Health Conditions," Centers for Disease Control and Prevention, April 29, 2021, https://www.cdc.gov/aging/publications/features/lonely-older-adults.html.

CHAPTER 5:

1. Rebecca Muller, "Here's Why We Should Celebrate Our Imperfections, According to a Psychologist," Thrive Global, April 16, 2019, https://thriveglobal.com/stories/celebrate-imperfections-social-psychology-expert-success/.

2. Thomas Curran and Andrew P. Hill, "Perfectionism Is Increasing Over Time," *Psychological Bulletin* 145, no. 4 (December 2017), 410–29.

3. Anna Sandoiu, "How Perfectionism Affects Your (Mental) Health," Medical NewsToday, October 12, 2018, https://www.medicalnewstoday.com/articles/323323#Living-with-a-harsh-inner-voice.

4. "Facts About Bullying," Stopbullying. gov, September 9, 2021, https://www.stopbullying.gov/resources/facts.

CHAPTER 6:

1. Olivia Hampton, "Allyson Felix Launches a Child Care Initiative for Athlete Moms," *Morning Edition*, June 21, 2022, https://www.npr.org/2022/06/21/1106261485/allyson-felix-launches-child-care-initiative-for-athlete-moms.

2. Simone Biles (@Simone_Biles), Twitter, July 23, 2021, https://twitter.com/Simone_Biles/status/1420561448883802118.

CHAPTER 7:

1. Jamil Bhanji and Mauricio Delgado, "Perceived Control Influences Neural Responses to Setbacks and Promotes Persistence," *Neuron* 83, no. 6 (September 2014), http://dx.doi.org/10.1016/j.neuron.2014.08.012.

CHAPTER 8:

1. Sara Eckel, "The Michelangelo Effect," *Psychology Today*, January 2019, https://www.psychologytoday.com/us/articles/201901/the-michelangelo-effect.

CHAPTER 9:

1. "Diverse Perspectives: People with Disabilities Fulfilling Your Business Goals," US Department of Labor, Office of Disability Employment Policy, accessed October 17, 2018, https://www.dol.gov/odep/pubs/fact/diverse.htm.

2. Anne Hathaway (@annehathaway), Instagram, November 5, 2020, https://www.instagram.com/tv/CHOGW7JlpRv/.

3. Ellen Pearson and Laura Misener, "Paralympians Still Don't Get the Kind of Media Attention They Deserves as Elite Athletes," The Conversation, September 1, 2021, https://theconversation.com/paralympians-still-dont-get-the-kind-of-media-attention-they-deserve-as-elite-athletes-166879.

4. Carla Filomena Silva et al., "The (In)validity of *Supercrip* Representation of Paralympian Athletes," *Journal of Sports & Social Issues* 36, no. 2 (January 26, 2012), https://journals.sagepub.com/doi/10.1177/0193723511433865.

5. Shira Springer, "7 Ways to Improve Coverage of Women's Sports," NiemanReports, January 7, 2019, https://niemanreports.org/articles/covering-womens-sports/.

6. "Woman in the Olympic and Paralympic Games," Women's Sports Foundation, June 2017, https://www.womenssportsfoundation.org/wp-content/uploads/2017/11/wsf-2016-olympic_paralympic-report-final.pdf.

7. "Our Research," Women's Sports Foundation, https://www.womenssportsfoundation.org/what-we-do/wsf-research/.

8. "Women in the 2020 Olympic and Paralympic Games," Women's Sports Foundation, April 2022, https://www.womenssportsfoundation.org/wp-content/uploads/2022/04/2020-Olympic-and-Paralympic-Report-1.pdf.

ABOUT THE AUTHOR

SCOUT BASSETT started playing sports at a young age as a way to assimilate into American culture. She tried basketball, softball, golf, and tennis before competitively racing in track & field. She is now an American sprinter and long jumper, holding seven national championship titles. In 2016 she represented the United States at the Paralympic Games in Rio, and in 2017 she was a World Championship medalist. In addition to her career as a professional athlete, Scout is an ambassador for the Challenged Athletes Foundation, a Women's Sports Foundation board member, and serves on the Gatorade Women's Advisory Board. She was a guest star on Project Runway, and has appeared in numerous campaigns for brands like Nike, Citi, Procter & Gamble, Bridgestone Tires, SKIMS, and more.